'He is courageously truthful about his own demons and pulls no punches in depicting his battles against racism. It's a terrific and, I think, important book' Salman Rushdie

'What fun!' Kate Moss

'Edward's journey is a lesson for the culture and future generations to come' Naomi Campbell

'Anyone interested in what it takes, from a beautiful human being's point of view, to change an industry from within, should read this book. Edward offers an insight only he can' Idris Elba

'Inspirational ... and it's not just for people in fashion' Claudia Winkleman

'The memoir tells the story of Enninful's meteoric rise' *Evening Standard*

'Inspiring ... I urge everyone to read it' Victoria Beckham

'He has been a pioneering force in bringing diversity (in all senses) to the pages of one of the most powerful magazines in the world, and now he shares his own story of triumph over adversity' Elizabeth Day

'Edward Enninful's keen eye for style has led him to dominate the world of European fashion magazines ... His latest mission is to share his barrier-breaking story' *Oprah Daily*

'Inspiring, entertaining, ground-breaking' Munroe Bergdorf

'The book he's written has power in it, and glamour, and humour, but also politics, and vulnerability, and a little horror too' *Observer Magazine*

'Edward Enninful inspires a whole new generation to show us anything is possible when you work hard with love and passion. This book is a revelation and shows the genius and strength of this wonderful, pioneering, legendary man of Fashion' Donatella Versace

'Despite all his hardships, it turns out he was born at exactly the right time, everything is changing and Edward has been an essential part of the fight' Grace Coddington

'Edward's book is the proof that you that you can have a beautiful soul, an extraordinary eye, and a loving heart... and confirms that showing vulnerability can be inspiring and glamorous!' Diane von Furstenberg

'Edward's story is a true beacon of inspiration, hope and change for the better. He has blazed a path for so many to follow, which sadly had never been possible before' Claudia Schiffer

'Edward is carrying out important work, leading change, and challenging the obsolete elements of the fashion system' Giorgio Armani

'Edward Enninful is not just a local hero but a globe icon' Steve McQueen

'A remarkable book' Krishnan Guru-Murthy

'A Visible Man is honest, illuminating, heartbreaking and funny – a beautiful book by a remarkable man' Afua Hirsch

'A Visible Man reveals a less than customary path to the pedigree world of glossy magazine' Grazia

'He is a serious man, on a serious mission; complacency is not in his vocabulary' Irish Examiner

'Cracking tale of a fashionista's rise' Telegraph

'A refreshingly intimate account of Enninful's rise from refugee status to editor-in-chief' Guardian

EDWARD ENNINFUL is editor-in-chief of British *Vogue* and the European Editorial Director for *Vogue*. As a lifelong advocate for diverse voices, Edward spearheaded 'The Black Issue' at *Vogue* Italia which featured only Black models. He eventually rose to become the fashion and style director of *W* magazine. In 2017, Edward became editor-in-chief of British *Vogue*, making him the only Black person to serve in this role in the history of *Vogue*. Born in Ghana, he currently resides in London.

A VISIBLE MAN

For my mother, Grace

EDWARD ENNINFUL

BLOOMSBURY

LONDON · OXFORD · NEW YORK · NEW DELHI · SYDNEY

BLOOMSBURY PUBLISHING
Bloomsbury Publishing Plc
50 Bedford Square, London, WC1B 3DP, UK
29 Earlsfort Terrace, Dublin 2, Ireland

BLOOMSBURY, BLOOMSBURY PUBLISHING and the Diana logo
are trademarks of Bloomsbury Publishing Plc

First published in Great Britain 2022
This edition published 2023
Copyright © Edward Enninful, 2022

A catalogue record for this book is available from the British Library.

ISBN: HB: 978-1-5266-4153-3; TPB: 978-1-5266-4154-0;
PB: 978-1-5266-4156-4; eBook: 978-1-5266-4155-7;
ePDF: 978-1-5266-4157-1
Waterstones Special Edition: 978-1-5266-5710-5

2 4 6 8 10 9 7 5 3 1

Typeset and designed by Office Of Craig

Printed and bound in Great Britain by CPI Group (UK) Ltd, Croydon CR0 4YY

MIX
Paper | Supporting
responsible forestry
FSC® C171272

To find out more about our authors and books visit
www.bloomsbury.com and sign up for our newsletters.

AMERICA

STEVEN

EVERYBODY RISE

MEGA-PHONE

PREFACE

One morning, during the early summer weeks of 2020, a time when London was eerily still and, even more strangely, sunny, I was in Hyde Park taking my Boston Terrier, Ru, on a socially distanced walk with a friend.

I was fired up. A pandemic was ripping through the world, bringing with it tragedy to countless people, and it seemed clear that societies across the globe were coming apart at the seams. Then in late May, I sat glued to my phone in horror, watching as George Floyd was murdered in Minneapolis. In the aftermath, the streets across five continents were filled with protesters. The world tilted on its axis as the most significant social justice movement in decades met the worst international health crisis in a century. I felt a familiar gnawing sensation within myself and shared with my friend that, after having been approached many times to write my memoirs, I'd finally agreed to do it. The world had stopped. Then it had exploded. It was time. It was also time for me, personally. I'd got to the point in my 34-year-long career where I could take stock of both my failures and my victories, and view them against the backdrop of a world I'd helped to change too, in my own way.

My friend, who, like me, grew up in an African household in the heart of London and had found great success in his own career, asked me what the book would be about. 'Oh, you know,' I sighed, 'a boy from Ghana making his way in a racist, classist industry, and the struggles along the way.'

He stopped me. 'Ed… nah, my brother. You move with leaders and tastemakers; you're surrounded by the most powerful, amazing women. We see glamour and swagger; we don't see a struggling Black person. Make sure you give us power and success. We need that.'

I was surprised by his perception. Like most immigrants – like most Black people, in fact – I didn't feel like I had 'made it'. Do you ever? Success for us is fragile, a fact that we have sadly come to appreciate more than most in the last few tumultuous and traumatic years.

The only thing I could say with any certainty about my life was that it had been driven by an all-consuming addiction to forward motion, and it still is. I had worked day into night in the fashion industry since I was sixteen, first modelling, then researching and hauling and steaming and putting in longer hours than were healthy. And I had certainly made an emotional investment in this calling that was not always fabulous for my mental health, either. Fashion shows, shoots, rejections, aggressions (both macro- and micro-), overnight flights and going straight to the studio, fittings, consultancies, making deadlines in the face of health and relationship and family sacrifices. I overachieved where others rested, ignored weekends, rarely took holidays and replied to every email I received straight away. (This last habit is one I picked up from Anna Wintour, incidentally.) It may all look glamorous from a distance – and yes, it has been filled with joys – but it has also felt like a ceaseless struggle.

So it took me a moment to see it from my friend's point of view, which was not what I had come through, but where

I had arrived at. Like me, this friend came from a place where his success was unlikely, the exception to the rule. He knew how important it was to provide models of joy and success for kids like us. But he hadn't lived my journey, and certainly didn't know all its contours, so he didn't yet fully understand why everything I'd experienced in my life was so critical to where I eventually ended up.

The question I am most often asked, especially by younger people, is: 'How did you do it?' At such a powerful crossroads of change, it felt like the right time to bring the answers even if, to be perfectly honest, I never saw myself as the type to write a memoir. By nature, I am rarely nostalgic. When, fresh from the printers, a new edition of British *Vogue* is placed on my desk each month, I don't spend much time dwelling over it, and certainly no time congratulating myself. Why look back when you can look forward? Why look in when you can look out? Where's the next evolution? I throw everything into my work, but once it's done, I'm really more concerned with what's new. The future is my thing.

It is this same energy that has propelled me through my life. I'm thankful for it. I didn't get to where I am – born on a military base in Ghana, where I spent my childhood, to the position of European editorial director of *Vogue* and editor-in-chief of British *Vogue* – by being unduly fascinated with myself. I embrace what's ahead, both by instinct and choice. Someone has to drag us into the future, I figured. I always wanted to be a part of that.

So it was that I found myself in Hyde Park that morning, chewing over the nature of the world and the story I wanted to tell in this book. The friend happened to be Idris Elba, the same dear friend who held my hand a year or so later while I cried tears of joy at my wedding, waiting for the minister to declare me married to Alec, my partner of more than twenty years, and now my beloved husband. We were in the Orangery of Longleat House in Wiltshire on a late winter's night, loaned to us by my friend Emma Thynn, Britain's first Black Marchioness, and her husband Ceawlin, the eighth Marquess of Bath. Our families were there, and dearest friends too. Everyone was beautifully dressed. White flowers heaved on the trellis, the grounds outside were lit by torches; the room was full of love. When the minister asked if anyone present knew of any reason why Alec and I couldn't be joined in matrimony, Rihanna, who was running late, burst through the back doors in a black lace dress, her pregnant belly resplendent. Through the tears, everyone burst into peals of laughter. Classic Rih.

I looked around the room that day at all those friends and family who had supported me throughout my life and saw my world in full focus. There were friends from fashion, Hollywood and beyond, but also many wonderful activists I had come to know and work alongside, the designers who had changed the way they do business, the editors and writers who had helped to lay the foundations for a new world in fashion that we built together.

Back at the beginning of the 1990s when I first started working in the industry, and even still, when I took over as editor-in-chief of British *Vogue* in 2017, no luxury publication wanted to have an ongoing conversation about diversity outside of the occasional special issue. My contention has always been that we need to be represented across all platforms as a matter of course. And by 'we' I mean anybody that has ever felt 'othered' by fashion, be that because of gender, race, class, financial status, body type, age, disability or simply having been denied a voice. Fashion is a mirror – sometimes a funhouse mirror, granted – of the world at large. The people who have found themselves on its outskirts here have usually found themselves on the outskirts elsewhere. It has been a personal mission of mine to change that. It is a mission that is by no means over.

Yet it is the only way I can ever have imagined doing things. I've always answered the question of what it means to create a magazine differently than most editors; to push harder, to dream bigger. Earlier this year, I turned fifty (on 22/2/22, no less), and where some in my cohort may start slowing down and enjoying the fruits of their long labours, I feel more energised than ever. Some in my generation have chafed at how digital publishing has forced us all to pull apart longstanding assumptions about communication, and embrace its many layers. Personally, I love it. Celluloid was a beautiful thing, but did I mourn the passing of its dominance? No. New technologies like digital photography, audio and video are opportunities to be seized. And that's just one example.

I may no longer be the outsider I was in my early career. I have become one of those gatekeepers who has seen his role evolve as traditional voices of authority have encountered a more democratic and accessible world through social media. To me, this evolution is a precious gift. Our audience can speak back to us now; why wouldn't we want to learn from what they have to say? Fashion's future depends on it. Anyway, as a Black person, frankly I think it's weird and a bit masochistic to fetishise the past. Things haven't always been so great for us, to say the least. There may be plenty in this world that's frightening, but I never feel frightened about the future.

Though I don't mind admitting I was a little bit frightened to write this memoir. My own story is inextricably bound up in my struggle to make fashion respond to the world, and in so doing, to help the world evolve too. It's only now that I have written this book that I see how, in working as hard as I have to force a reckoning in fashion, I have also forced a reckoning within.

I'm not normally given to revealing myself. I'm private by nature, especially when it comes to the difficult stuff. But my hope is that I can do something for the future if I tell the story of my past. I've always told young people who asked about my life and career: 'If I can do it, you can too.' It's important to me to inspire them, because the world as it is isn't set up to do that – it's quite the opposite, in fact. And yet, we need young people coming into the world as empowered as they possibly can be. They are the ones who will help us all get somewhere better than we could have done alone. More than anything, I have written this book for them.

GHANA

Tema, 1979. Clockwise from top:
My sisters Mina and Akua, our cousin Sasha,
and me, aged seven.

CHAPTER
ONE

Sometimes, when I'm poring over a newly arrived set of photographs on the computer in my home office at 6 a.m., or I'm huddled with a photographer and a superstar model on set past midnight with three more looks left to shoot, I feel at my most content. Through bougie Western eyes, this probably looks out of balance: I'm overworking at the expense of my personal life; I need to create boundaries, or whatever. But I've never seen work and life as truly separate. It's not how I was raised. My parents were both hard workers; their careers were at the centre of their lives. Even as they were surrounded by six kids and an endless extended family, nobody went hungry. And I've been my parents' son since the day I was born, at the tail end of a dry African winter in 1972.

I can't imagine any other line of work for my father, Major Crosby Enninful, than the military, with its authoritarian rigour and devotion to order. By the time I was born, the Ghanaian military was one of the most powerful in all of Africa, and it made for a prestigious career. Officers had solid, middle-class lives, with houses on military bases and enough pay to ensure education and upward mobility for their children. Kwame Nkrumah, Ghana's first president, the first in Africa to sever his nation from the British Empire, had a pan-Africanist vision for the country that was once known as the Gold Coast. As Ghana was relatively socially and economically advanced among its neighbours, it meant that Ghanaian soldiers traditionally did frequent tours abroad, often aiding United Nations Peacekeeping forces. So, for most of my childhood, whether he was in Liberia, or Egypt or the Middle East, my father was elsewhere.

That suited his children just fine.

I was born in Takoradi, one of the bigger port cities along the coastline, the fifth of what would become a family of six children. There was Crosby, the eldest, named after our father, my sister Mina, brothers Luther and Kenneth, and baby sister Akua. In Ghana, it's common to take the name of the day on which you were born. As I was born near midnight on 22 February, the hospital had one date, and the post office another. So my mother Grace gave me two Ghanaian names: Kobina Kweku, or Tuesday Wednesday, as well as my Christian name, Edward. I was really only Edward in school. Most people called me Asiamah. In Akan, the country's most dominant language after English, it means 'Blessed Child'.

We lived on a military base in Takoradi, a cocoon of pristine order inside the more laid-back city. The base was dotted with neat little stucco bungalows on stilts that we used to run and hide underneath. When I was still quite little, we relocated from Takoradi to the capital city of Accra, where we lived on another base called Burma Camp, just across the road from the sea. It was a similar dynamic: our family living on an island of tidiness surrounded by a city unconcerned by order. Burma Camp looked so organised and perfect to me as a child, with its clipped lawns and freshly painted little houses.

That order hid a darker reality. Ghana suffered from political instability and frequent military coups. Whoever was in charge at the time was often settling scores with whoever came before. Our home was the last in a cluster of cottages, and we had a clear view of a hill that had a string of wooden posts erected on top. That was where they'd execute, by firing squad, whoever was considered an enemy of the state. Every few weeks or so we could see it happening from the window of our house: the soldiers would march condemned men with pomp and ceremony, cover their heads with hoods, take aim and fire. We'd hear the gunshots crack as their bodies would slump. 'Oh, is it firing-squad day?' we'd ask each other. Anything habitual becomes normal when you're a kid.

We had a lot of space in Burma Camp, with five bedrooms to shelter my siblings and me, who ran in a pack together. I was the baby until 1977, when Akua was born, so most of the time, everyone took care of me. Much of it involved keeping away from our father, who was a believer in distributive justice – if one of us acted out of line, we all got yelled at. Or worse, we'd get the leather strap on our hands. As we were constantly making noise, we spent a lot of time at the beach, playing in the sand, and taking part in deadly serious track-and-field competitions. I was a shy kid but a good student and confident in my abilities – I'd end up skipping two grades before I got to secondary school – so I'd show other neighbourhood kids how to do maths on the beach with rocks. They would call me 'teacher'.

I was, above all, watchful, shy, spacey, and totally consumed by my imagination. Some days, as my brothers ran about kicking up sand, I would find a quiet spot and take those same rocks and turn them into a pretend class of my own. Each rock became a character. I'd dole out praise, correct their mistakes. I would sass them and make jokes at their expense. When I was in my comfort zone with my brothers and sisters at home, no adults to yell at me, I felt free. When I had my confidence up, I found joy in making people laugh, even the older kids.

When I remember my childhood, its powerful scents come rushing back to me first. The sea air and fried fish, which we'd eat with fermented corn dumplings called kenkey, and hot peppers. In Ghana, you buy groceries either from the central market if you're in a larger city, or on the street from trailers, which were all over, loaded with vegetables and fruit and peanuts, colourful and abundant and waiting to be turned into something delicious. In stalls they'd sell grilled turkey tails, which are just the end of the bird, crispy and loaded with fat. I remember the smell of bodies close by at the crowded markets, the air full of spices. Fish and meat would sit out on display in the muggy air, while fierce women strolled by carrying massive pots of soup on their heads, their babies strapped to their backs.

Ghanaian cuisine is often starchy – my grandmother's specialty was fufu: pounded cassava and plantain dumplings, which she'd make with a massive, waist-sized mortar and pestle. You'd dip the fufu into fragrant, peppery soups. Ghana's climate is mostly tropical, with a summer monsoon, and anyone who comes from a tropical part of the world knows that spicy, high-temperature food is an important part of cooling the body down. I still eat hot pepper with every meal, no matter my location. There is a lot of depth of flavour in our cuisine, much of which we have in common with our West African neighbours. Stews are full of beef, fish, crab, chicken and shrimp, sometimes all together, and layered with dried shrimp powder, bitter herbs and peanut flour, spiked with tomatoes and chillies and onions and lime. My nose always knows if I'm visiting someone from Ghana from the smell of that cooking – there are a lot of us in London – and every time, it takes me back home.

The coastal cities in Ghana were well developed, but the countryside was another story. When I was really little, my mother would take us to visit my grandmother in her tiny village of Brakwa, in a forest belt about sixty miles from the coast. She lived in a small, squat house fashioned from mud and cement block, which had no electricity. The drive on dusty, red-clay roads was rough and bumpy. When we'd get there, I would have to say hello to all of my aunts and cousins and grandmother's friends. There could be fifty of them, because my grandmother was like royalty in that town, and everyone had to show respect. It was scary in those little houses, especially once the sun went down and left us in the dark. Even though I held my mother's hand, as a visitor I felt poked and prodded by curious hands. I kept my head down and wished it would be over soon so I could get back to our comfortable house and my books and drawings and records.

I was coddled by my mother, brothers and sisters, and in their company I was happy, though sometimes I was in excruciating physical pain. I was born with the blood disorder sickle cell trait (and then later diagnosed with a related disorder, thalassaemia), which means my blood cells form a kind of hook that doesn't flow well into the tiny vessels in my joints. When my condition flares up, as it does from stress, or poor diet, or, today, taking a lot of aeroplanes, it's like having an especially piercing case of arthritis and only morphine can really take the pain away. Because of this, I bounced back and forth to hospitals to have my blood checked. My mother would always be there with me as the doctors did their work. Because I had more of these attacks when I was younger, I could never be too far from her. I have so many early memories of her arguing with doctors, pleading with them to do something to ease the pain. Much less was understood about the disorder than is known today, and even as a tiny boy, I could feel my mother's worry and frustration that we had to keep coming back to the hospital over and over. Why did this pain keep coming back? She couldn't understand what was wrong with her baby, much less make it stop.

My mother was my comforter and my champion, and a formative example for me of courage and the power of the imagination. In Brakwa, when she was just a teenager, one of twenty-two kids (as is typical in extended polygamous African families), she started making dresses for the local ladies. She had an amazing eye for colour and, as she honed her skill, a talent for fitted shapes. A few of her brothers became tailors, too, so perhaps awareness of clothes runs in our family. At seventeen, my mother assembled her best samples and travelled from her village to the capital of Accra to try to get a place at a technical college. At the interview, they told her not to bother – she already knew everything they could teach her, anyway. And so she picked up and moved to the north of Ghana, still a teenager, to a Sahelian region that's a lot more Muslim than the Christian coast, to set up a dressmaking business. That's where she met my father.

Major Crosby Enninful's military duties made him a sporadic presence around our house. As severe as the black suits he wore when he was out of uniform, he would appear, terrorise us, and leave. When he was around, the party was over. 'Don't play, your father's home!' was the refrain. His children were supposed to be studying. He might have been a highly ranked soldier, but he was fighting a battle with his kids that he'd never ultimately win. He'd rail against my eldest brother Crosby, his namesake, a bad boy, a smoker. He was gorgeous in his cut-off jeans shorts and bright yellow shirts, and girls followed him around everywhere. According to my father, Crosby was going to ruin us. (Today, he's an Anglican minister, and as serene as my sister Mina.) Crosby would play Luther Vandross and Evelyn 'Champagne' King records around the house. 'What you do to me is a shame! Ooh, gonna love you just the same. . .' He was ten years older than me and so seemed like this force of coolness from another planet.

Mina was next in line, a radiantly beautiful junior version of my mother: loving, gentle and kind. Mina sees the good in everyone. Just thinking about her now makes me well up. Then came Luther, who was my absolute hero, so engaging and handsome, with that same infectious charisma that Crosby has. Luther loved sharp dressing even when we were kids, though he really came into his own when we got to London. Kenneth was next, brainy and studious, but also kind of a jock – a picture of success from a very young age. My father's favourite, Kenneth always wanted to be a doctor, though illness prevented him from completing his studies. He's living in Ghana today in a happy relationship with a devoutly religious woman. I loved my siblings, and they mostly took good care of me, though they couldn't keep their hands off my food. In Ghana, it's the grown-ups who get the biggest and best portions, and the littlest who have to fend for themselves. The minute I'd turn my back, someone would dive-bomb my plate and steal the one piece of meat I had on it. I had to hunch over my plate if I wanted to eat anything without scavengers. It wasn't just at home, either. If we were at the beach, it was open season on my ice cream. Luther was the worst of them all.

There were exceptions to my father's perpetual scowl. Sometimes he'd come home with a few friends for beer or palm wine – the fizzy, sweet homebrew served just about everywhere in West Africa. He'd be in a good mood, possibly induced by whatever was in his glass, and would send for Luther and Kenneth to come out and dance. They'd bop around to a few songs — everybody listened to American music back then, in our house mostly soul and R&B and jazz — till he'd excuse them and back to bed they'd go. At least he was laughing.

Crosby, Kenneth and Luther all loved to play football, which they'd do almost without fail every day when they were together. But then someone would get wind that our father was on his way home and they'd rush back in to clean the red-clay dirt off their feet and legs before he walked through the door and caught them out for the crime of kicking a ball around. He reserved his sweetness for Mina, of whom he was very protective. She was the only one of us kids who got a ride to and from school in his car when she was younger — she suspects because by picking her up as soon as class let out, she couldn't get into trouble. And later on, the truest apple of his eye was our sister Akua, whose stubborn tenacity rivals his. (Before I put aside all freelance work to become editor of *Vogue*, Akua was my agent. I picked her for a reason.) But to us boys, he rarely had a nice word to say.

Some of my father's rigour is simply cultural. African families are often a lot larger than typical Western nuclear families, and so being able to establish discipline and respect for authority can be a survival skill for parents. But he was our biggest source of fear as kids, and the rejection I felt in particular, because I was shy and more artistic and sensitive than my brothers, would keep us from developing any kind of an affectionate connection until much later in life. It wasn't just that I felt he didn't understand me; I felt he actively disdained me.

Even when I was young and didn't have the language to explain it, there was always a tension between how I might want to act naturally and what my father considered appropriate behaviour. I learned to check my every instinct when I was around him, though luckily I didn't internalise his disapproval to such an extent that it entirely killed my spirit. I just learned to hide. Even when I was little, I was good at impressions and would have my siblings in stitches mimicking all the local characters from around the neighbourhood or on the radio. But I'd never have dared to shine a spotlight on myself in his presence. One day, I wanted to wear my mum's shoes just for fun, as little boys sometimes do. (Or at least this little boy did, fascinated as he was by her style, and ladies' style in general.) I was walking about around the neighbourhood with my brothers, just doing my thing in a sensible midi-heel, no big deal, when, out of nowhere, one of the more savage stray dogs that prowled around our house bounded out, barking and chasing. It wasn't even an elaborate stiletto, but it was enough to impair my getaway skills and I fell and got a nasty bite. Out of the question that my father knew any details around why I fell. (I was terrified of dogs for years and years afterwards because of that bite, even more than I was of my father. Thankfully, my love of heels never suffered from the association.)

My mother eventually tired of life at Burma Camp. She almost certainly tired of death at Burma Camp as well. The sound of executions happening like clockwork weigh heavily when you know what it means. There was another change of government soon in the offing, and perhaps the ongoing reminder of how fluid political favour could be finally wore her down. She wasn't going to be like the other military families who packed up and moved all the time, either. The military might have been how her husband found his way in the world, but thanks to her talent and ingenuity, she could take more control over our family matters. With her business, she could give us a greater level of stability than would have been possible if my father had been the sole breadwinner. So when I was eight, the family moved off base into a pair of houses in Tema, the largest seaport town in Ghana.

At Burma Camp we were spread out over five bedrooms, and still my father would complain about the noise. Now we would all be squeezed into two, in the first house there. Ceiling fans rotated endlessly to clear the crushing humidity in the simple, sparsely furnished living room. A television was what counted for décor. Despite what I do for a living, the apartment I share today with Alec bears a similar asceticism. I have the same aversion to excessive home décor as my parents. (Mina does too.) For all the truly unbelievable pictures I've been part of creating over the years, most of those that I've kept and framed are still leaning stacked up against the walls because I just don't want that much visual distraction. (I will confess that my *Time* cover was framed and hung on the wall in record time. And I have a few other photos from collaborators like Steven Meisel, Juergen Teller, Emma Summerton and Craig McDean. And sure, when Beyoncé sent me a framed print of her British *Vogue* cover, there was a space over my dining table for that one.) As soon as I was able to move out of flatshares into my own place, I've opted for calm.

Where I'm from it's normal for four kids to share a bedroom, and everyone sleeps on straw mats on the floor, as we did in one of the two bedrooms in our family house in Tema. I loved that way of sleeping, and felt so safe. Our grandmother, whom my mother had by then convinced to leave Brakwa to come help take care of us, had the other bedroom. One of its walls was stacked high with suitcases that held all of our stuff. I adored my grandmother, who would cook us anything we asked for on demand. We weren't overflowing with toys, though our mother's older sister, Aunt Bertha, would sometimes refresh our supply. She was strict and demanding and scary, with a temperament a little more like my father's than my mother's, but she worked in the customs office where she was the frequent recipient of favours (small bribes, one imagines). Sometimes she'd pass them along to us.

I was more interested in books. If Crosby, and later Luther, turned us all on to music, already by that age, I was the family librarian. Having already read everything in the house, I'd borrow whatever I could from friends at school, read it as fast as I could and then circulate to the rest of my siblings so they could do the same. In Ghana, there was no TV until six o'clock at night, at which point we were supposed to be doing homework, so reading was a much bigger part of our entertainment than I'd imagine it was for middle-class kids in the West. I could get into almost anything, from *Snow White* to the *Hardy Boys* and *Nancy Drew* to Ian Fleming and, later, the thriller writer James Hadley Chase. I was a precocious student and always found the time.

But as much as I loved books, I loved clothes even more. When Luther would come home from boarding school for holidays, and his smart school uniform of white shirts and shorts would be washed and made crisp again, I'd be the first person to get at them. I had to look sharp, as I was my mother's chief assistant.

The other house in Tema was my mother's atelier. By then she had a serious dressmaking business, with thirty to forty seamstresses working under her at any given time. While my father never wore a colour or pattern in his life, the clothes my mother made were fabulous, combining Western fabrics and traditional West African wax cotton prints in riotous colours with an enormous variety of styles. She had a flair for drama and volume, with peplums and bell sleeves. Her tailoring was precise. West African women's clothing is typically quite structured, built to hug and flatter curves, and my mother mastered it.

She made dresses and suits for actresses, society ladies and wives of diplomats and heads of state. From 1972 to 1978, before he too was deposed in a coup, the president was Ignatius Acheampong, and his wife was one of my mother's favourite clients. I'd go with her for fittings to the presidential palace, with its high stone walls and air conditioner blasting. She liked my help, as I knew how to keep quiet and behave. And she liked that I took an interest in what she did. She had notebooks filled with sketches, and she'd also often work on loose-leaf paper, dividing one sheet into nine squares, drawing a different look inside each. I'd imitate her all the time, and still do today when I'm brainstorming an editorial of multiple pages, grabbing a sheet of paper and drawing those same nine squares.

I clung to my mother's skirts as a child, and as I got older, I still spent as much time as I could in her workshop. That's one place I discovered how fashion really works. My mother was discreet with her clients, quiet and shy. She'd show them fabrics and take their measurements and together they'd decide on an idea. She was incredibly focused on running her business, but she was also dreamy, and often somewhere else in spirit. (I'll never forget one time when, tagging along with her in London in our old neighbourhood of Ladbroke Grove, she just started walking out into traffic. I had to pull her back from getting hit by a car.) When her clients came in for their fittings, or when she'd go to their homes, I'd be there, just as silent and serious, to help my mother zip them in. I learned how to fasten a hook and eye without pawing someone, and how clothing works technically on a woman's body. I saw from my mother's example how to talk to women about clothes and work with them to come to new ideas. I learned to recognise the expression on a woman's face when she turns to look at herself in a new dress and finds what she sees really beautiful. And also how she knows when it's not quite right. You can imagine how this has come in handy as a stylist. These days, Rihanna or Taylor Swift need only move a millimetre of their faces for me to know if it's love or hate.

I was transported by the whole experience of the workshop: the colours, the fabrics, the loving attention of my mother and her staff. It lit up my imagination. I'd sit under my mother's cutting table, surrounded by scraps of wax fabric, and fill my own notebooks with ladies in elaborate dresses like she did. I'd show them to the seamstresses and they would pat my head and compliment me, 'This one is so good, Asiamah! Look at that sleeve!' Then someone would warn me that my father was coming, and I'd have to hide everything. He hated my drawings and hated that I wanted to draw. The same notebooks I filled with flights of fancy, so full of enthusiasm, I'd then burn so he wouldn't ever find them. It was unfair. I loved glamour and women and their style and was drawn to them instinctively. I never imagined then that I'd make a career out of fashion – it never occurred to me until I was much older that it was even a possibility. But what was wrong with being inspired, especially by something that brought my mother so much success? What's good for the goose was not good for the gander, as far as my father was concerned. Creative careers were for women, apparently. The Enninful boys would be doctors and lawyers: respectable, distinguished, cerebral, credentialled, dull.

In Tema, one of my aunts had a hair salon called Dolly Dots. It was in the Meridian Hotel, which was brand new at the time, in a neighbourhood called Community One. The Communities of Tema are kind of like tiny boroughs.

We lived in Community Two, which wasn't remarkable one way or another: rows of little square houses, kids playing in the street, stray dogs and cats here and there, just to keep things interesting. Community Six was where the rich people lived, in big mansions with tropical gardens. Community One was just being constructed then, and I would trek through fields of tall grass to find the hotel. Today it's squalid, but when it was new, the Meridian was incredibly posh to my young eyes. Dolly Dots was a tiny slice of a space in the lobby, painted black, with mirrors and colour photographs of chic Black hair looks and standalone hair dryers and ladies just waiting to be transformed. If I wasn't in my mother's atelier after school, much of the time I was here. I'd show up all by myself in the lobby and head straight in.

I loved my aunt, and I felt totally at home in that very female space, but I wasn't there for the hair. I was there for the magazines. Every month, she would have *Ebony*, *Jet* and *Time* delivered. It was a big deal in Ghana to get American magazines. I'd devour the photos of Diana Ross and Jayne Kennedy and Donna Summer and the Somali model Iman. All these fabulous Black goddesses in fantasy settings, or in career looks, or on the beach, their eyes fixed on the camera. I felt their eyes connect with mine, like they were looking right at me. I would sketch them in asymmetrical off-the-shoulder dresses, teased hair and a block heel.

A small aside on the risks inherent in meeting your heroines: years later I would go on to work with one of the great Black divas, whom I had been dreaming about in some way or other my whole life, for an advertising job for a big cosmetics company, in New York. I had used all my resources and favours to pull pieces from all over the world so that she might be impressed by the professionalism of me, the Black stylist from London. I wanted it to be perfect for her. Preparation is the key to styling, and I thought I had turned it out. This superstar arrived at the studio, I introduced myself and walked her over to a room with twelve racks of dresses and tables of accessories ready to be loved. Through her sunglasses, she scanned the room from the doorway, declared, 'I hate everything,' and walked off. (I know you're dying for me to say who this woman is, but I believe stylists should have confidentiality codes as rigid as doctors do. And in general, I don't believe in trashing people in public forums.) Counterpoint: At around the same time, I also got to work with Iman for the first time, on an advertising job for Tommy Hilfiger, with her husband David Bowie. They were both huge influences on me, and were radiant and generous and a joy to work with. To see how they made each other laugh will stay with me for ever.

When I could, I'd bring the magazines home like precious jewels to share with my siblings. Later on in life, after I started working for *i-D*, more of my siblings ended up working in fashion — Mina was scouted by a model agent when she was away at university in Calgary, Luther went to cordwainers' school and worked with me a bit in my earliest days as a stylist, and Akua went on to become not just my agent, but one for other prominent stylists and photographers too. Though Akua and I were the only ones to really stick with it, I like to think of us as a small tribe, our sensitivity to clothes and style moulded by our mother. I never really felt myself as a family leader, though I suppose I was.

In 1978, President Acheampong, who himself came to power in a coup, was overthrown in another coup by Frederick Akuffo, the head of his armed forces. Less than a year later, Jerry Rawlings, an Air Force lieutenant with a reformer's streak, overthrew Akuffo, who was promptly executed. Corruption has been an issue in the country since before the Gold Coast became Ghana, and banging on about it was an easy way for populist leaders like Rawlings to gain support. For two years, a politically moderate civilian government was in charge, and then Rawlings made another move and took over as head of the country in 1981.

It started to become clear, little by little, that it wasn't safe for us. With so many coups, people naturally belonged to different political families, and our family was not part of Rawlings's. That was enough. A cousin of my father's, Colonel Joseph Enninful, had presided over the military trial in 1979 that convicted Rawlings of mutiny. Rawlings escaped justice, and a few months later, some of his supporters came to Joseph Enninful's house and shot him and his wife dead at the breakfast table. Someone called our house when it happened. At first we thought they were taking about our father, and we were terrified until we heard from him. Around the same time, the fathers of two of Mina's friends at school were executed. Suddenly, we weren't allowed to play outside as much and had to be home a lot more often. I was petrified to leave the house anyway, and entertained myself in my little world in the atelier. Trips to Dolly Dots were now out of the question. It was hell on the older kids too. Anyone who was seen to be living too well was suddenly under suspicion. There was tension in the air that turned into something scarier. Nobody knew any more who was friendly and who wasn't when you passed them in the street. Images of my father getting marched up the hill at Burma Camp plagued me.

As my childhood freedom became locked down, it was my turn to go to boarding school. Even if the country was reeling, people clung to anything that felt normal. I hated the idea of leaving my mother and the atelier, but at least I'd catch a break from my father's aggressive manner. In Ghana, kids from middle-class families are typically sent to boarding school at fourteen. As I had skipped a couple grades, I was only twelve when I enrolled in Adisadel College, where Kenneth was already attending. It was – still is – a prestigious boys' school. Ghana has always had a strong, serious academic culture, and earning a place at Adisadel, one of the top ten boys' schools in all of Africa, was proof you could be elite. It had a sprawling campus on Cape Coast, about four and a half hours away from Tema by car, with ten student houses around which social life was organised, like the British public schools after which it was modelled. Modelled, but with a Ghanaian touch: ivy doesn't grow in Equatorial Africa. Our dormitories were whitewashed stucco blocks on stilts, unadorned and functional. While we wore white dress shirts, black shorts and black-and-white-striped ties during the week, or black-and-white-striped, short-sleeved dress shirts on Sundays and for ceremonial occasions, students would also don white collarless cotton shirts and drape themselves in togas made of vibrant Kente cloth. Adisadel's original name was St Nicholas, and so we students were known as the Santaclausians. 'Play up! Play up Santaclausians!' went the cheer we were encouraged to sing during inter-house football matches, not that I went to many. I preferred track and field, and ran the 100-metre dash. It was a good way to forget the tension back in the big city.

Ghanaian schools are rigorous and disciplinarian. It's not uncommon for primary-school kids to get the strap. But throw a bunch of boys together and no matter what, you're going to get hijinks. At Adisadel we slept on squeaky iron beds in big open rooms, so if someone was getting up at night to sneak around, everybody heard it. There was a lot of hazing. As I was younger and shy, I was a prime candidate for harassment. I only escaped it due to Kenneth, who was older, wiser, and most importantly, very, very popular. I'd eat my porridge in the morning with the rest of the kids, and do my schoolwork in peace.

Because I was away from home, I was even more removed from the danger that faced my family. The situation simmered until it exploded, and my father suddenly said goodbye and left for England. At first I thought he had simply abandoned us, because I didn't understand the bigger picture and no one talked to kids about that kind of stuff. His departure seemed like a punk move, but I had such a low opinion of the man that I just rolled my eyes and found another reason to curse him. One day when I was home on a break a few weeks later, the road to the presidential palace was overrun. Then, maybe two months after that, Kenneth and I came home from school and all the other kids were jumping around, excited. 'We're going to London!' London? Where all the pop stars I had read about came from? Amazing!

London was the place everyone wanted to be. There was a kind of reverence around it, to the point that one summer a few years before, when Kenneth and I went to stay with a family friend for a month, we were barred from sitting at the dinner table with some other guests who had just come from London. They were that special.

My mother needed to stay behind to wrap things up with her business, so it fell to my brother Crosby to get us organised for the trip. If she was worried for herself, or for us, she didn't show it. She was busy but kept cool and calm, one imagines, for us. We got all dressed up for the journey, in traditional African dress clothes: tunics over long pants for the boys and a wax-print dress for Akua. (By this time, Mina was already attending university in Calgary.) We packed as much as we could as quickly as we could and headed for the airport, with my mother treating it like a big adventure for us.

In the time between when my father left Ghana and we met him in London, he was put up in a little residence in Lancaster Gate, not far from where Alec and I live now, and worked to ensure us safe passage. Applying for asylum in the United Kingdom takes a long time, but apparently it was bad enough in Ghana that we couldn't wait, so my first trip on a plane was under conditions far more harrowing than I really knew. We took Ghana Airways, all seated together in a row, a bit forward from the smoking section. All I really remember was thinking the aeroplane was cool, and helping to keep Akua, who was just seven, entertained. When we finally arrived at Gatwick Airport, we were detained for hours, all together, as they checked our papers.

There was a big problem: we didn't have any. As members of the British Commonwealth, Ghanaians didn't need visas to travel to the United Kingdom until just before our journey, when Margaret Thatcher changed the rules. Because the rule change was recent, we were able to get out of the country without everything in order, but upon arriving in the UK, all together like the West African Jackson Five with baby Janet, we were stuck until our father could come out on the train to present what paperwork he had.

During all the waiting and the nervousness and the not knowing what was going to happen, they fed us dinner

— for some reason it was turkey, and it wasn't terrible, even if it wasn't how we were used to eating it back home. As we ate this weird food, and gawked, and poked each other, and whispered, my brothers and I were struck over and over by how strange it was.

Oh my God, we said to each other. It's all white people.

LONDON

London, 1988. At age 16,
my glasses had finally come off.

CHAPTER
TWO

I don't think I'd ever been as happy to see my father as when he came to pick us up at Gatwick Airport and took us to what would be our first home in London, a tiny three-bedroom flat belonging to our Auntie Baaba in Vauxhall. Since we had left our mother back in Ghana, it was only when we saw our father in his black suit, and the visible relief on his face, that we had some sense of stability and home in this totally unknown place. Even if home with him meant a lot of tiptoeing and lectures.

Our eyes were hungry for the novelty of this strange-looking land as we sat together wide-eyed, staring out the windows of the train. It was a lot to take in as we bounced around with excitement, overwhelmed at the thrilling coldness and greyness of absolutely everything. We'd never seen a place laid out with such rigorous logic and uniformity. As we wended our way from the airport to our new home, not far from the Thames, across the river from Westminster, the suburbs became the city. The buildings seemed so old to me, the architecture so grand and imposing, so brown and red. We'd seen pictures but had never actually seen brick buildings in real life. We didn't even know what bricks were! To us, London felt like a more consequential form of Disneyland – picturesque, foreign, surreal.

Let's not sugarcoat it, though. While I was delighted with the novelty of it all, the Vauxhall neighbourhood where we landed was pretty shabby in 1985, with street after street of rundown Victorian houses, council flats and industrial concrete, roaring roads and soggy skies. The brutalist blocks, purpose-built as low-income council estates, filled empty spaces left by the Blitz's bombs forty years earlier. Back then, along with working-class Londoners and Portuguese, African and Caribbean immigrants, Vauxhall was home to a fairly thriving squat scene. All that life and chaos created a totally new soundscape of sirens and people and double-decker buses roaring through the rain-soaked streets. What would our mother think, once she finally arrived? And when was that going to happen, anyway? And meanwhile, what would become of us here? How would we get along? Would the people be nice to us?

In retrospect, I just have to laugh. Black people who grew up in Africa often have a different relationship to white people than Black people who grew up in places where white people once held their ancestors in bondage. Although we all came from societies recovering from the aftermath of colonialism in some way, most Black Britons at that time were of Caribbean descent, the progeny of people who had been enslaved, and then migrated to Britain where they lived in a white-run world. They knew that the deck was stacked against them practically from the minute they were born.

Our formative years couldn't have been more different. As African immigrants, families like ours did not have the horror of enslavement as part of our narrative. In Ghana in the 1970s and 80s, the colonialists were gone – from visible power at least – as was the British Imperial government. Despite various lingering quirks of the old regime, and the very real control British companies retained over Ghana's rich mineral assets, the Empire simply wasn't part of the mindset of my generation. There were a few white people in Ghana, but they were welcome. We loved their different accents, and understood that if they had actually come to make a life there, it was because they had a feeling for us too. Sure, we were sometimes bemused by white people, but we never felt threatened by them. We had the confidence of knowing we were equals. More than that, we were hosts. They were on our turf, and since most of them meant us no harm, all was well.

The same was not the case once we got onto their turf, where we were seen as interlopers with our hands out, ready to cause trouble. Beyond the excitement of our emigration, we knew we had escaped danger because of how suddenly we left our home. What we didn't know yet was that, arriving slap-bang in the middle of London in the 1980s, we'd landed into danger of a more insidious kind, one that would set our lives on a different course and make our opportunities more of a challenge to claim. We had left a home where we were part of the majority for a place where our futures would be proscribed based on the colour of our skin, our accents, and, for all the discourse of the new Commonwealth, our 'foreign' customs. I've had endless conversations with British-born Black friends who speak of growing up with a certain fluency in incredibly complex, racialised situations: they found the behaviour of white people sometimes outrageous, occasionally devastating, almost always puzzling. In Ghana, we had the luxury of never thinking in terms of black and white. For all its excitement, our arrival in London put a full stop to that fantasy. We showed up excited to be in the glittering home of cool pop stars and the Queen, and landed into Margaret Thatcher's hateful mess.

Days after we first turned the key in Auntie Baaba's door, Brixton, the heartland of Black Britain, just down the road from us in Vauxhall, burst into flames.

In the 1980s, the United Kingdom was heavily polarised, its racial tensions egged on by the flinty-eyed, hairspray-helmeted Conservative prime minister, Thatcher, who was known for going on the BBC and breathily intoning right-wing zingers such as: 'If we went on as we are. . . by the end of the century there would be four million people of the new Commonwealth or Pakistan here. . . People are really rather afraid that this country might be swamped by people with a different culture.' Ghastly. Never mind that many of those who came over from the new Commonwealth and Pakistan as economic migrants were coming from former British colonies, where the ancestors of people like Thatcher swamped *them*, with far more violent and mendacious intent. Surely it was the people from what became the colonies who had the right to hold a grudge over the treatment they received both back home and in the UK, when in fact all they were doing was trying to share in the abundance of ancestral wealth that their free labour had created? For that, they were treated as criminals, an invading force in danger of overrunning the country.

Britain's immigration panic had started in the 1950s and 60s, as the post-war economy needed bodies for manual labour. The population of colour really did grow rapidly at that time, with people coming from the Caribbean, India and Pakistan, Ghana and Nigeria. By the time my family got to London, it had already started to become the multiracial, multi-ethnic city that it is today, but that state of affairs didn't go down well with everyone. Thatcher and her cohort's demagoguery, aided by the willing and all-too-able establishment media with a vice-like control on the nation's attention, succeeded in stirring up white resentment up and down the social classes. We were still kids when we arrived, our heads spinning, and the subtleties of people's reactions to us, and all of this context were still mysterious. But when our father watched the news at night, and yelled back at the prime minister, we knew even then that things were not exactly copacetic. On-screen, with her pussy-bow blouses and that tired, fussy little handbag never far from reach, she made her poisonous fascism-lite easier to bear by leaning into her 'middle-class grandmother' identity.

All around us were the signs of Thatcher's cruel and repressive policies, issued under the guise of fighting crime and carried out by a particularly aggressive police force. Brixton was a working-class neighbourhood where almost half of the population were Black. Its residents understood from experience that the police behaved differently there than they did in, say, Kensington and Chelsea, where old money flowed and most of the people were of a paler hue. Though the British police aren't militarised like the American police, excessive force against Black Britons is still an epidemic, and it was even worse then. At the time, London's police had a policy colloquially referred to as the 'sus law'. It was similar to New York City's recently cancelled 'stop and frisk', meaning police were legally empowered to stop, question and search anyone they deemed suspicious. The criteria were totally subjective, as the mere fact of being Black in public – walking, talking, hanging out, alone but especially in groups – was often seen as suspicious. So Brixton had had quite enough of the unjust, demanding, often violent end of the law by the time we arrived. Its residents were well and truly sick of it. Even as a relatively clueless young teenager, just by being Black and in that space, I knew what side I was on.

There had already been spectacular civil unrest in the neighbourhood a few years before our arrival. In 1981, an investigation into a house fire due east of Brixton in New Cross, which killed a group of Black kids, ascribed little to no blame where it was due. Demonstration statistics are notoriously hard to pin down, but many thousands of people showed up to protest, mostly peacefully. Nevertheless, the police crackdown was brutal, and as a result, violence exploded. Our father followed the news of that first unrest back in Ghana, even though to us kids then, it was distant and abstract. While he vocally supported the uprising when the topic arose, it was just a headline to us, nothing more.

A few years later, when it happened again, we were in more of a position to understand. At dawn on 28 September, 1985, police burst into the Brixton home of Cherry Groce, a single mother of six. Seeking her son Michael, who was under suspicion of robbery, they shot her in front of three of her children. (The name Breonna Taylor, the medical technician from Kentucky who was shot by police in her home in March 2020, will probably come to mind, and make you wonder if there are any new stories. Unlike Taylor, Mrs Groce survived the violence, though as a paraplegic in constant pain. She died in 2011 of kidney failure at the age of sixty-three, and it took another four years for an inquest to declare that her death was premature as a result of the wounds she suffered in that raid.)

When word of Mrs Groce's shooting got out around the neighbourhood, people poured into the streets. Windows were broken, cars were overturned. The police came charging in with riot gear as rocks and Molotov cocktails were thrown and anything flammable was set on fire. We were ordered not to leave the house as sirens blared down the street, but we could see the sky change colour out of the window at Auntie Baaba's flat. Over fifty were injured and 200 arrested that time, not quite as high a toll as the first uprising, but, due to the repetition, it made just as many headlines. Brixton was the first time I saw with my own eyes how badly Black people in Britain are treated. There have been many, many more reminders since.

As I write this, some corners of the British media have just commemorated the fortieth anniversary of the first Brixton uprising. 'Without the uprising in Brixton you wouldn't have had Black people elected to parliament in 1987,' the Black Labour MP Diane Abbott told the *Guardian*. 'If you tried to talk about racial justice in the early eighties, you were just dismissed by those on the right of politics, even on the right of the Labour party, as someone with a chip on their shoulder.' Today, we do have Black MPs and a civic language to address our grievances. After the killing of George Floyd in 2020, Boris Johnson's right-wing government issued an independent Commission on Race and Ethnic Disparities, whose findings it then promptly rewrote to downplay their seriousness. Meanwhile, data from the Office for National Statistics showed that in the same year, 41.6 per cent of Black Britons between the ages of sixteen and twenty-four were unemployed, compared to 12.4 per cent of white ones. It's crucial to have political representation, but results are what count.

We may have landed into another kind of war zone, and as newly minted Black Britons we were starting to understand that there were targets on our backs, but we had escaped the Ghanaian goon squads coming to march us up the hill at Burma Camp. Our family was safe and holding strong those first months in Vauxhall. For fancy Londoners, before the gentrification wave came in the 1990s, the whole of Lambeth, the larger borough Vauxhall was nestled in, was synonymous with urban blight. But we didn't know any fancy Londoners. To them, it was the hood; to us it was lively, with music and the occasional familiar food smell wafting out of a window, and other Black people everywhere we looked. Not every Black person we saw in the street was Ghanaian, with our familiar points of reference, but their presence around us was something we were starting to realise was important to our sense of well-being.

Like all asylum seekers, my father wasn't allowed to work for three years after his arrival. It was unpleasant to have him around the house all day long, where he scoured the newspapers for news of back home. He'd brood and we'd just try to get on with it. He had saved a bit of money and received a small stipend, but it wasn't enough for us to get our own flat without government help. While we waited for our living situation to get sorted out, all five of us kids (Mina was still at university in Canada), plus my father, wedged ourselves into my generous aunt's tiny home. She worked in a garment factory in East London, and already shared the place with her two daughters Angeli and Darling, and a cousin, Stephen. With our arrival, everything was upended. The boys and my father got one room. Akua joined her girl cousins in another, and my aunt held onto the last room for herself. As we were used to sleeping with many kids in a single room in Ghana, nothing about this setup fazed us, especially as we were still getting our bearings. We'd put our mattresses down on the floor at night and hoist them up against the wall when we needed room to circulate. It required organisation, a skill we had all more or less acquired to spare us our father's wrath. This sort of arrangement happens all the time in immigrant neighbourhoods when new family members arrive from back home. We were still wide-eyed from the novelty. We took solace in our family, and we were mostly having a fantastic time.

My brothers and Akua and I were thrilled by the busy-ness and noise and density of London. When my father would send us to Tesco to do the weekly shopping, it is no exaggeration to say it was like touring Willy Wonka's chocolate factory. I was obsessed. We'd never seen a supermarket before, so crammed with perfectly organised, brightly wrapped treasures. We'd run down the aisles gleefully tossing chocolate digestives and Lilt, an ambrosial fizzy pineapple and grapefruit drink, into the trolley. Chocolate was never personally my thing, but as I grew older and stopped being able to eat and drink anything I liked without consequence, fizzy drinks like Lilt were the hardest habit to break.

We had a whole list of weekly chores established by my father. Every Saturday, all the kids assembled to clean the flat. Because I was still relatively little, doing dishes was usually my lot, or sweeping out the space, including the patio that ran along the length of the flat. Since my aunt worked full time and we had no spare grandmother like the one we'd left back in Ghana, soon it fell to Luther to cook for everyone. Out of the question that my father would do it. He was busy watching football and yelling at us to be quiet and do our homework. With our aunt's help, and then later our mother's, Luther became really good at kenkey and fufu and all the dishes we ate back home. My aunt would stand over him, instructing him how and why to cut the onions a certain way, or when to add the meat, and then he started to get the hang of it. Years later, when Luther had moved in with a girlfriend and had a daughter of his own, he'd still come by the family house to cook for everyone.

Because there were so many of us, at mealtimes we all just grabbed a seat where we could, with our plates on our laps. I can't eat much traditional Ghanaian food unless I want to blow up like a balloon, but I miss it so much I find myself spending hours on Instagram looking at plates of fried tilapia and shrimp swimming in all those gorgeous spicy sauces. It's like an express train to my childhood, when everything seemed a lot simpler.

At dinner time we'd all cluster around the television set and watch *Dynasty* or whatever British sitcoms were popular at the time. There was one called *In Sickness and in Health*, which featured a Black, gay home-care worker named Winston who was nicknamed 'Marigold' by the gruff but supposedly lovable protagonists. I just remember thinking, my God, how revolting and tired. Is this what people here think is funny? Or Benny Hill, the national treasure, who ran around in blackface as if it were the cleverest thing in the world? To us he was just a buffoon.

At home, we still acted as if we were in Ghana, but when we were out of the house, we were in the UK, and the climate of London took getting used to. As September turned into October and November, the weather began to get colder, and suddenly we started wondering if we wouldn't be better off still in Accra. (Ask anyone who's lived their whole life in a warm climate how they handled the cold for the first time. It's an extreme feeling and, along with a collection of second-hand ski jackets and scratchy wool jumpers, you have to build up defences.) The first time we saw vapour coming out of our mouths on a cold day, we didn't even know what it was. Someone, maybe it was Kenneth, theorised that it was sulphur because we had just eaten eggs.

For Luther, Kenneth and me, our father chose Lilian Baylis Technology School in Vauxhall, and I'm grateful to him for it every day. Its student body of eleven- to nineteen-year-olds was almost entirely Black and Southeast Asian. He never said as much, but I think he knew that being at a school with other kids of colour would cushion the blow of repatriating and adjusting to everything else about life in the UK.

Lilian Baylis occupied a massive brown-brick campus by the Thames, built in that blocky post-war style. It was considered a rough school where gangs circulated, a source of concern for the hand-wringing powers that be, even if every year plenty of kids there also tested well and moved on to better things. The Tube passed overhead; the classrooms were damp and a little musty, but it had a multimedia lab and its own basketball courts and a running track. Back in Ghana, we had to read about science experiments; here we could actually take part in them. What did we care about the noise from the Tube? It was still exotic and modern and glamorous to us. In that first year, I still harboured my infantile dream of becoming an Egyptologist, which was far too impractical for my father to encourage. Of course, when I stammered that interest out to anyone, they'd laugh. Like, does this Black African boy actually think he's going to study the continent? That's for white scientists, as evidenced by all the pillage still on display in the British Museum.

The kids there called recently arrived African immigrants 'Boo Boo', so that was how Luther, Kenneth and I became known. I never really hung out with the boys. Most of them were too rough for my taste, and I had my brothers, anyway. But there were three girls whom I adored, and who could call me Boo Boo any time they liked: June Bailey, Dawn Kelliot and Anne-Marie Johnson. All three of them from West Indian families, they were instantly legendary to me. June was probably my first idea of a muse. She was stunning: mid-tone, with her hair always pulled back tight. Sade was the big style inspiration at the time, with her tight ponytails and big hoop earrings, and these girls rocked the look. In retrospect, the largeness of the hoops bordered on the insane, but that's what made them fierce. They wore bomber jackets, pencil skirts and penny loafers, so they'd sort of waddle when they walked along. They were confident and feisty and they loved shy, sensitive, polite me, who became a mascot for them. I was smitten.

So often, there is a sacred bond between queer kids and the straight girls who support them. It's primordial, and certainly for me was tacit, because I did not know myself that I was gay or even think of the world in those terms back then. Too scary. Too adult and illicit. Yet Lilian Baylis is where I first consciously realised that women were my special weakness in a way that felt more important, more nourishing, than simply wanting to kiss them like the other boys did. Especially big, fierce women. I was in awe of a coach who was athletic and strong and dark-skinned, a bit like Serena Williams. She would bark at the kids and we all knew who was boss, and I just ate it all up. My ardour for these women wasn't sexual, but it was and is passionately felt. Back in Ghana, all the time I was drawing women, going to Dolly Dots to thumb through magazines filled with them and helping my mother to dress them, I didn't really think about it. I was young, I was helping my mother, and nothing about it seemed weird. But here, in London, everything was different – the cityscape, the weather, the accents, the noise and the people. And apparently, my view of girls and women. The boys at Lilian Baylis often treated them horribly. They teased the girls, insulted them, talked down to them, objectified and ignored them, as if they were foreign objects with no ideas or feelings of their own. They were missing out on all this treasure right under their noses.

Lilian Baylis was also where I got my first real political education beyond my father's running commentary at home. I went from a boys' boarding school in Ghana with a distinctly authoritarian culture, where they'd use canes on students who stepped out of line, to a place where we'd all sit in a circle, boys and girls, and talk about literature and laugh. The older students were encouraged to question the text, rather than memorise it. I was too shy to misbehave and my manners were still pretty formal, as my African upbringing required. But I liked the spirit and the ease about it and flourished in that more open context.

We already knew that for our father, only one of the noble professions would do for us kids. So we had to perform well in studies that would put us on track to become doctors or lawyers. Because I was a naturally gifted student, and had already skipped years, I had no problem with science and maths, so I could play the game. My strategy was to get those subjects out of the way so I could spend my time on subjects I preferred, like art and literature. (My Egyptology fantasy bit the dust pretty fast.) I always read anything I could get my hands on, but at Lilian Baylis I started to really appreciate poetry. Maya Angelou's 'Still I Rise' was and still is one of my favourites, though I've read and loved everything she's written. When I was asked by my head teacher to contribute to a book of poetry, I wrote something obviously inspired by Angelou, about the Black struggle. We had an open day to celebrate the book, and my teacher told my dad I was a brilliant student. He kept that book for a long time. Even if I always felt his existential disapproval of me, when I attained worldly achievements that clicked with his standards, he celebrated them.

As hungry as I was for knowledge at school, my obsession with style and music was even stronger. Not long after arriving in London I started hanging around the magazine rack, looking through *Vogue* and *Harper's & Queen* (now *Harper's Bazaar*), but also *Blitz* and *Smash Hits* and *Number One* all afternoon. I realised that if I walked in with a crap magazine from home, I could put it down on the shelves and take a new one, so I did that all the time. Boy George, Spandau Ballet and all the New Romantics, their singers like pretty, exotic birds, were in their pomp, and the pages of those magazines seemed to shimmer with the promise of nights out and great outfits and energy. And these were almost within reach. I mean, I was in London. Look how far I'd already travelled. Why not me too, one day? I loved those eighties music magazines and devoured the New Romantics' music as much as the latest R&B and soul. I am not unaware of the irony of having gone from swiping magazines in my adolescence to making a career in them. Let's just say those glossy pages have been an ongoing source of value to me.

Three months after we first wedged into my aunt's flat, our father secured one of our own, at Cheylesmore House, across from Chelsea Barracks in Belgravia. Ironic that we left barracks life in Ghana only to sit across from barracks here, though these soldiers were white, and rough, and we were not part of their world. Though it was across the river on the fancier side of the Thames from Vauxhall, the council flat was hardly posh. Still, the difference in this upscale, genteel neighbourhood from where we first arrived was stark.

Like lots of teenagers in London at the time, Luther and Kenneth got jobs doing a paper round. This meant getting up at five in the morning and going to the newsagent near Sloane Square, picking up an armload, dropping them off one by one on doorsteps all around the King's Road and Chelsea Embankment, and getting back home in time to go to school. Even though I was too young at thirteen to be taken on by the newsagent, I tagged along anyway. What else was I going to do: stay in bed while my brothers were out and about? Unthinkable. The newsagent's was run by an elderly Indian couple who were sweet to us. Maybe they felt for us as immigrants, just as they once were. 'Bye bye, dolly,' the wife would say to us over the tinkling bell as we left the shop, so that's what we came to call her. My brothers each got something like £35 a week from Bye-Bye-Dolly for the work; Kenneth would give me a share of it for my help.

It was on those paper runs, roaming around Sloane Square, one of the poshest areas in London where many of my friends live these days, that I got my first indelible taste of how it felt to be the other in my adopted country. It was not just a white neighbourhood: it was the home of the infamous Sloane Rangers, the old-money girls best represented by Diana, Princess of Wales. The Enninful boys stood out like peppercorns in a bag of rice. Though we didn't run into many residents because of the early hour, when we did, we'd often catch a suspicious look, as if we had invaded their inner sanctum and were poised to defile it by the mere fact of our presence. God forbid we were heard laughing amongst ourselves, as we often were. To their eyes we were clearly no longer young enough to be deserving of charity and kind looks, but passing into the age of juvenile delinquency. Sometimes kids from the neighbourhood would chase my brothers and me, yelling at us to go back to Africa. How were we supposed to get back to Africa when our father wouldn't even let us out of the house after school? Heaven help the Sloanes, we were such a menace to society. If we weren't on the paper runs, we had to come straight home and do our homework, no friends allowed.

The flat at Cheylesmore House was even smaller than my aunt's, just three tiny bedrooms and an even tinier living room, bathroom and a kitchen. We weren't there for more than a year, when, after what seemed an eternity, the door opened and, finally, our mother walked through. Our father had gone to the airport to get her, just as he had done for us what seemed like a lifetime ago. We waited at home in anticipation for the key to turn in the door. When they came into the flat, we all rushed at once to hug our mother. Our father must have felt like the odd one out; all of us kids were so enamoured of her. And never more so than at this moment, when we had been under his thumb for months without her kindness and gentleness to help us take on this new country and culture. Our parents weren't loud arguers, but I'd sometimes overhear my father complaining to her about 'you and your kids'. When he'd hector me for doing something spacey or creative or soft, he'd use phrases like 'you and your mother'. Now she was back, and it was such an especially joyful reunion for me. On some level he had to have taken our unbridled celebration as an indictment on his own parenting.

Life in London was as different for my mother as it was for the rest of us, but it had to have been a ruder shock, even if she never showed it. Rather than directing a staff of forty and dressing the wives of presidents, she was taking under-the-table commissions from friends and extended family, which she would sew herself. But she was essentially upbeat and grateful by nature. She'd never complain, even when her wrists and back would get stiff and sore after hours of straight work. We needed the money – my father still wasn't permitted to work; nor was she, and we were used to having some level of comfort back in Ghana. Technically, she wasn't supposed to do it, but she had a skill and, more importantly, she needed to do it. Making clothes was a structured outlet for her imagination, which was a lot like mine, constantly in the service of beauty and style and glamour. And, like me, she needed to occupy herself.

With such a reduced business, she didn't need my help like she did when I was much littler. And I was working hard at school and still struggling to fit in. After our first physical separation, now I was feeling a second separation. I was out and about and, naturally, didn't need her apron strings quite so much.

We established a new rhythm in the flat, accompanied by the loud clacking of my mother's sewing machine, and cousins coming in and out, eating Luther's cooking. We'd pop in to say hello to her when we got home from school, or on breaks from homework while my father would be drinking a Guinness and talking about football. Crosby got a car, so he was gone more often than he was home, which left Luther, Kenneth and me to absorb our father's lectures. But on the weekends, I regressed in the happiest way. My mother had friends who were working at Brixton Market, so every Saturday, I'd go there with her to do the shopping. There were a few stalls run by Ghanaians that were like being back in Accra, with the same cuts of meat, and peppers and fish and kenkey. Bob Marley and Peter Tosh were always playing over the loudspeakers and to this day, when I hear their music, it takes me back to those weekends when I was so relieved to be back at my mother's side again.

A year after her return, in 1987, we finally got to move into a council house in Ladbroke Grove. This is what we had been waiting for. It was next door to a Turkish bath that would end up, ten years later, becoming the Cobden Club, a very chic private members' bar where I'd often go with Naomi Campbell and Kate Moss. Even in the era of the Cobden Club Ladbroke Grove was a slightly rough neighbourhood, but in 1987, it was downright scruffy. While our house was being built, we'd catch the Tube from Sloane Square in Belgravia and watch it coming up, imagining what it would be. Finally we found out: spacious, with five bedrooms, including one for Mina, who was finishing up university. Her room was at the back of the main floor, next to my parents' room and the living room and kitchen. Then downstairs there was a bedroom for Luther, Kenneth and me, and another for Akua and a family friend called Sasha, and eventually what became a workroom for my mother, where she'd have clients come and visit for fittings. Then Michael Boadi, a friend of Kenneth's from Adisadel, came to stay too, because he was having a rough time with his father, who had emigrated years before we did, and was a devout Christian. We'd put Michael's mattress down near the top of our three when it was time to sleep. There were nine of us under this roof, and it felt palatial.

Michael's father was already naturalised in the UK, so even though he was the same age as me, Michael knew London and how it worked better than I did, and who was cool and not cool. He was a valuable resource for someone still as shy as I was outside my family, with my big Afro and glasses, who just didn't want to get noticed even as I was noticing everything I could that was going on around me. Well, perhaps I wanted to get noticed a little. At night, with our parents upstairs, Kenneth, Luther, Michael and I would talk late into the night about movies or the TV shows we were watching along with everyone else in London, like *EastEnders* or *Neighbours*, the Australian soap starring Kylie Minogue that seemed to have the entire UK entranced. (It was a simpler time.) In those years, Michael and I became especially close, developing a kind of secret language, just the two of us, over fashion and hair. It took me another few years to realise what we shared was a budding gay sensibility, though Michael knew sooner than I did.

Kenneth remained the closest to me in all things, but Luther became another conduit of cool once we were in London, just as he had been in Ghana. He was so handsome and engaging that everywhere we'd go people would stop him and ask him to be in things. He started passing time around King's Road and became friends with people who hung out with the boy band Bros, who had some pretty big hits around then. The stars of the band were two stunning white brothers, Luke and Matt Goss, and their style was sort of James Dean, with faded jeans and cowboy boots, but with a sheen of 1980s excess. It was a look Luther adopted as well. He could have passed for one of the members of the Pasadenas, a Black British pop group with hot-combed hair and matching Perfecto leather biker jackets. He'd get his used Levi's from Portobello Market and taper them on our mother's sewing machine. Luther would let me tag along with him, which, in retrospect, was incredibly kind, as I did not cut anywhere near as stylish a figure. But that is how African families roll. All for one and one for all.

In the UK, when you turn sixteen, you sit your GCSEs. If you pass, you can then decide to join the working world, attend a technical school to learn a trade, or go on to higher education. If you opt for higher education, as my father had made clear was to be my path, the next phase is called sixth form, to study for A levels, and then go on to university. For sixth form, I enrolled at Kingsway College, in King's Cross, ostensibly to prepare to become a lawyer, a career path about which I couldn't care less.

Taking a page from Luther's book, I had decided college was not about my Lilian Baylis look of flat-front, second-hand pants and second-thought jumpers. I had finally shaved off the sides of my Afro and had persuaded my mother to let me get contact lenses and vintage jeans like Luther's. Not to be too *She's All That*, but this was the first proper butterfly moment in my life. Apparently, it made me attractive, because one morning on my way to college, reading *Blitz* magazine on the Tube, an unassuming-looking white man with a shaved head couldn't stop staring at me. Stop after stop, I'd look up over the edge of *Blitz*, and there he'd still be. Finally, at Baker Street, it was time to get off the train, and as I did, so did he. Then he started talking. He told me he saw me reading *Blitz*, so he knew I liked fashion, and asked if I would ever be interested in modelling. He handed me his card and introduced himself as Simon Foxton. I didn't know it yet, but more than almost anyone else in the world, Simon would change my life.

i-D

London, 1991. Posing for Nick Knight.

CHAPTER THREE

I suppose I did look a little different on the Tube that day — a little different from how I felt inside, anyway. My inner self was still catching up with the outer me. What Simon Foxton spotted on the Hammersmith & City line was not the awkward refugee kid from Africa. What he saw was the Ladbroke Grove teen I was becoming.

It's hard to point to a setting in other cities that compares to the neighbourhood I had by then lived in for just a couple of years. There was a special, electric kind of energy in Ladbroke Grove. I suppose it was a little bit like the East Village in New York or how Kreuzberg in Berlin would become in the 1990s, except it was even more diverse and polyvalent. It wasn't just one scene or social group that ruled, but a jumble of working-class immigrants. With mostly derelict buildings, graffiti, dilapidated terraces and council estates to look at, Ladbroke Grove was not quite as pretty as some of the nearby garden neighbourhoods like Holland Park, with its enormous white houses that looked like wedding cakes lining streets, which seemed straight out of *Mary Poppins*. Other than the odd quaint corner of bricks and flowers, Ladbroke Grove's aesthetic appeal was in its people. Cool, crumbling and sprinkled with just the right amount of crazy, in Ladbroke Grove you really felt like anything, or anyone, could come along and change your life in a minute. It was a place where you were as likely to see an It Girl buying her Diet Coke and Silk Cut in the corner shop in the morning as you were to be mugged outside it at nightfall.

I was desperately absorbing new styles and new ideas — maybe not yet daring enough to try them all on myself, but I was cataloguing every look and every kind of person that corresponded to it. I was just old enough and had been around London long enough by the time we moved to Ladbroke Grove that I was finally able to analyse and understand the social and dress cues of my fellow Londoners, which I lapped up with the hunger of a fast learner looking to find his place. 'Show me your outfit and I'll show you who you are' is how I'd people-watch back then. What was happening in Ladbroke Grove had me wide-eyed. I loved it the minute I stepped out of our front door on Kensal Road each day. And now I was old enough and, apparently, cute enough to start to imagine that I could fit in.

I had a lot of banners to choose from in Ladbroke Grove. Everyone felt themselves in the neighbourhood, and they often made a statement. A lot of the West Indian families had come over a generation before, so their kids who were my age acted fly and confident, like they owned the city, or at least the neighbourhood. There were still a few old-school punks, bless them, clinging on to the hair dye and piercings long after the explosion had petered out, and ska boys with their poker-straight, three-quarter-length trousers with a knife crease down the front, and an absolute drove of beardy types wearing sandals and batik trousers in all weathers, who looked like they should be juggling on a beach somewhere, even if they were just in the queue for the post office on a wet Wednesday. Peppered among them, alarmingly but so thrillingly, came the alternative sexualities whose queerness seemed woven into every stitch of their clothes. In Ghana we didn't have a Western concept of gay and straight – in Tema we never thought there was anything strange about our neighbourhood's transgender prostitute, Ashawo, glamorous with her handbags on her way to meet the sailors from England and Germany. She was kind to us and we loved her. But here there were identifiably gay men with giant moustaches and aviator sunglasses and the tiniest shorts you've ever seen, or ripped sweatshirts, ankle boots and jeans so spray-on they provided an anatomy class all on their own. Outside the Tube or in the parks, they would cluster together as if on a team. Black girls with the latest-shaped Afros would be out doing errands with their headscarved mothers, passing by crusty Communist Party militants selling the *Morning Star* on the street. It was a kaleidoscope of wildly coloured track suits, army jackets, bangles up the arm, dreadlocks, beanies and a lot of stickers that read 'Free Nelson Mandela', after the song by the Special AKA.

There was no internet, so being in the right place at the right time was everything. There was no hiding in your room if you wanted any sort of life, even if you were shy like me. If you wanted to know about clubs, you had to eavesdrop around Kensington Market, or look for fliers in the record shops. Luther and Michael and I definitely wanted to know about clubs.

Unlike the King's Road, where every good trend went to die, style in Ladbroke Grove was about realness and identity. If you wanted to express any sort of individuality, it began on the streets and it started with what you wore. You got creative because you had to – most of us had no money, so we haunted vintage shops, and slashed, cut, patched, tapered, shredded and bleached our surplus gear. There was a market called Hyper Hyper, which was opposite a really cheap, buzzy shop called Sign of the Times, where you could get rubber shirts or creepers, if that's what you were going for. I'd spend hours at Honest John's, an indie record shop, checking out rare, groove records in the listening booth. I may have been gawking at pictures of Boy George since before I landed on British shores, but the first album I ever bought, at Honest John's, was *Whitney Houston*. (I can listen to anything, but I am at heart an R&B boy. If you love me, give me Betty Wright.)

Ladbroke Grove was it, and its spirit had no greater apex every year than the Notting Hill Carnival. The parade's endpoint was near our then-council estate on Kensal Road. A street party like no other, certainly not in the UK, it's got the thumping music, impeccable vibes, sequins, feathers, jerk chicken, beer buzzes (buzzes of every kind) and energy you'd find in any Caribbean country before Lent strikes.

Today the Notting Hill Carnival is an expression of cultural pride and necessary hedonism, but it started in 1959 as a gesture of appeasement, as the situation for the growing numbers of people of colour in London had started sliding into shit. Hoping to heal wounds suffered in the first-ever so-called 'race riots' on home soil, which happened the year before, when racist Teddy Boys firebombed the homes of Black

Notting Hill residents, the editor of a local West Indian paper got approval to organise a Caribbean-style indoor party with steel drums and a beauty queen crowned at the end of the night. As that party became a standing yearly appointment for the neighbourhood's large West Indian population, the hippies and their local outdoor free festival joined forces with them. The Notting Hill Carnival as such was born like a parliamentary alliance of subcultures looking to stake out a demilitarised zone where the city's alternative communities could hang out and drink and smoke spliffs and get up to no good, all together. Very Ladbroke Grove.

My young head exploded the first year I went, which must have been the year we first arrived. It was all the jiggly women in big headdresses and sequinned bras. Such a fashion moment! African women tend to dress more modestly than Caribbean women, and at the Notting Hill Carnival was the first time I saw so many beautiful Black women really letting it all hang out. Belly buttons. Cleavage. Samba dancing. I was in heaven. Over the years, violence flared up every now and again at the celebration – the police didn't learn the lessons of Brixton and never stopped antagonising the Black community of Ladbroke Grove – but we never missed it. If I'm in London during Carnival, it's unthinkable to me not to be there.

So there I was, sixteen, very shy and still following Luther and Michael's leads, but little by little, I was starting to gain independence and confidence. Ladbroke Grove was the perfect place for a young person without any money to attempt different looks and identities, as there was already an example of just about everything. Where Michael, who was living with us full time for a spell, went for skin-tight jeans and T-shirts worn with booties and hot-combed hair, like a sort of warmed-over Revolution-era Prince, I was desperate for Luther-style leather bomber jackets and destroyed Levi's and cowboy boots, or military surplus. Anything that felt epic and a bit hard that I could mix with the American trend associated with Bobby Brown and Teddy Riley and the whole New Jack Swing clique – monochrome or colour-blocked velvet dress jackets with proper shoulders. One big moment was when, at sixteen, I bought my first pair of cowboy boots at a store on the King's Road called R-Soles. (Say it fast, with a British accent.) They had them arranged in rows according to colour all up and down the wall. True to form, I got black ones. Even then I liked very masculine and minimalist codes for myself, which I freely admit was due to my father's sober and elegant personal style. All dressed up, we found places to go. We'd get a bunch of my cousins together and go east to Dingwall's in Camden, a bar that played rare groove and acid jazz. I was learning how to dance listening to pirate radio around the house with my brothers, and it turned out that I was good at it.

Looking back on our nascent personal style, it was heavily influenced by the Buffalo movement. Buffalo had been canonised a few years earlier, in the mid-1980s, by a stylist called Ray Petri. He hung out at the Lisboa Café, around the corner from our family's council estate. We knew who he was and would gawk at him smoking outside, with his long, chiselled face, in his MA-1 leather flight jacket on the arm of his square-jawed muse, the British-Burmese model Barry Kamen. Petri had a stall in the Portobello Market, but he came to fame as a stylist. One story he did for *The Face* magazine a few years before in 1985, shot in crisp black and white by the photographer Jamie Morgan, was key. A then-unknown Naomi Campbell, who couldn't have been more than fifteen, appeared in it in an oversized black blazer with shoulders out to there, alongside Barry Kamen and a thirteen-year-old cockney kid called Felix kitted out in a bowler hat with the word 'killer' emblazoned across the front and a scowl. Petri also worked a lot with the photographer Mark Lebon, who shot for *i-D* all the time and had an apartment across the road from my family's council house. About the same time that Simon Foxton gave me his card, Neneh Cherry turned the rest of the world onto Buffalo with 'Buffalo Stance'. Petri was by then too ill from AIDS to style the video himself, so handed the project off to Judy Blame, a former Blitz-kid scenester and protégé of his. Against a tie-dyed backdrop, with Cherry in bike shorts, a gold bomber jacket and a dollar-sign neckpiece, the video had all the pop and colour and brashness of its namesake.

Though Buffalo's name came from Bob Marley's song 'Buffalo Soldier', and it had its truly pop moment in music thanks to Cherry, it was first and foremost a fashion idea that took strong shapes and pieces loaded with outward significance – a bowler, a trench, a kilt – and placed them on unexpected people. Motifs from the American West or Scottish Highlands or professional boxing or the Royal Family would be put on unlikely models, to play with and beautify and question mainstream standards. It was very street-real, informed by the legacy of punk, but also the unique alchemy of Ladbroke Grove, refined by Petri's brilliant editing. Buffalo co-opted symbols of strength for people who most of the world weren't used to seeing claim ownership of anything. That, and its confident mix of masculinity and femininity, made it highly sophisticated as well as in-your-face. Ray Petri's work was classical and streamlined. There was the symbology and multiculturalism, but Petri also pinned and belted and gathered and ruched like a Grecian sculptor. He was the first proper stylist as we've come to know the term today: someone who told stories in images through clothes. But Buffalo also had its impact because of his attention to detail and gift with line.

You could say that Luther's Bros clique, in their cowboy boots and shredded Levi's, were dressing in a distillation of Buffalo. Though sophisticated, there was a top note of sex that was hard to ignore. On a personal level, as well as an aesthetic one, Ray Petri had a thing for men of colour. In photoshoots that he conceived – for what is a stylist but an ideas machine who is constantly suggesting story concepts to photographers? – Petri showed mixed-race men like Barry and his brother Nick, and Simon de Montford, whom he scouted working at a fruit stand, with depth and dignity and complexity of mood. It's not surprising that, along with a ton of other Ladbroke Grove kids at the time, Luther and I found ourselves in that style.

If Ray Petri was one of the buzziest stylists in London, before 'being a stylist' was really a thing, Simon Foxton was the other. I didn't know who or how important he was when he gave me his card, but Michael, who was starting to pick up work in hair salons, had heard of him, as had my friend Rowan, whom I met at Kingsway College and who did a bit of modelling as well.

Pop culture during the 1980s was pulsating with energy and ideas, and with that came the arrival of London's highly influential independent fashion magazines. Their pages were filled with the stars of the underground style and arts scenes, and they'd sit nestled right below *Vogue* and *Country Life* on the shelves of the local newsagents, easy to discover. *i-D* launched in 1980, the same year as *The Face*, but where *The Face* was more music and culture, *i-D* had a fashion focus. It was founded by Terry Jones, a one-time enfant terrible art director, after he had had enough of his job at British *Vogue*. Terry was fascinated by the punk scene and London street fashion in general. He had a revolutionary's eye, a talent for arresting, punchy imagery and lived in horror of becoming an institution. Terry wanted an outlet to document and interpret what he saw all around him, outside the strictures of the rigidly commercial fashion media. So he went and created his own magazine where he could indulge his own fetishes: reworking images and adding whole new signatures in post-production, whether through collage, layers of colour or film reprocessing. *i-D* printed its first few issues in a shop that normally pressed badges for punks and politicos. I had certainly heard of *i-D* when Simon gave me his card, even if I wasn't reading it regularly. With my introduction to him, that immediately changed.

i-D was the closest you could come then to a pure documentary of British youth and their culture tribes. Terry worked frequently with the photographer Mark Lebon, who had a poetic approach to naturalism and, like Terry, loved roughing up raw film. As alternative as the magazine was, it was also cheeky and cheerful and in on the joke. Since its inception, every model on the cover has been shown winking in some way or other. And its priorities changed with the times. The new direction we found in the 1990s, when I eventually came to work there as an editor, was not the one it had when it started, nor the one it has found now. But it was (and still is) ultimately a celebration of the creativity of young people.

i-D could offer such authority on youth because it was primarily staffed by them. Terry, the ultimate cool dad, became famous over the years for finding promising kids and trusting them with both responsibility and freedom. He had a great eye for spotting talent and the ability to nurture it without micromanaging and snuffing out a person's spark. He'd send photo students off with only the most threadbare budgets to shoot some fashion story or capture some rock star in the wild, and in return, he let people experiment and explore their own aesthetic fascinations. He rewarded good work and loyalty by promoting from within.

Now that I'm in a position to staff and run a magazine myself, I'm grateful every day that Terry was my founding example in the industry. The talent he put together was astounding. *i-D*'s long-time editor, Dylan Jones, started his career there before going on to edit British *GQ*. Terry pulled Caryn Franklin, the activist and fashion historian who went on to create *The Clothes Show* for the BBC, out of academia to put her to work on the magazine. Nick Knight, the brilliant photographer and impresario behind SHOWstudio, was still a student too when Terry started commissioning him. Judy Blame was mostly a jewellery designer when he started styling for *i-D* with Mark Lebon; those two went on to practically create a whole new aesthetic of their own. A lot of people came and went over the years, but the core was very loyal, like a family.

Simon was *i-D*'s men's fashion editor, but he had started out as a designer, having earned his degree at Central Saint Martins, the art and fashion school that shot out new talent like a firehose starting in the 1980s. (Its students from that period included Lee McQueen, John Galliano, Stella McCartney, to name just a few.) Simon and Terry had first bonded while Terry was also creative director of the New Wave sportswear company Fiorucci. In the early 1980s, he engaged Simon and Vivienne Westwood, the doyenne of punk fashion, to do separate collections backed by owner Elio Fiorucci. Neither collection went anywhere, though Terry recognised a gift in Simon and put him to work. (Vivienne Westwood didn't ultimately need his help, though *i-D* was always a great supporter.)

Like Ray Petri, Simon had a thing for Black men, both as romantic partners and as photographic subjects. He stopped me, he told me later, because I reminded him of Djimon Hounsou, the dark-skinned Beninese model who broke out in Janet Jackson's 'Love Will Never Do Without You' video. Thanks to the influence of Petri and Simon – integral parts of *i-D* and *The Face* – and the rising success of MTV, male models, and in particular Black male models, were having a moment. Simon was, like Ray Petri, a great pioneer of street casting, pulling in everyday people like me with an interesting look to star in photoshoots. This kind of casting usually goes exactly as it did with me, to this day. You spot someone on the street, or in a shop or on the bus, show them a copy of the magazine, and start talking to them to get a sense of their energy and spirit and how they move. If you like what you see, if they give off a kind of spark that makes you want to know more, you take a Polaroid, exchange contact information, and go from there.

Even if I was a kid on the Tube when Simon gave me his card, everything about the moment felt right, as well as thrilling. Of course, then I had to come down to earth and think practically. If I wanted to model, I'd have to get my parents' consent. Kingsway College was going well. I was getting good marks, as I always did, studying English literature, sociology and politics, even if my chief interests were now clothes and clubs. There shouldn't have been any reason for me not to model, except my father was not the most approving type. So I skipped my father entirely and asked my mother as soon as I got home that day. I showed her Simon's card. She took it and turned it over, seemingly unimpressed. 'The fashion industry is full of funny people,' she said, looking me dead in the eye. I realised she meant gay. I didn't see how that concerned me. I wasn't gay. No ma'am, not me. No way. Simon was the first out gay person I had ever even met.

My mother loved me and understood me, and she could see this was important to me. Or rather, I made her see, because I pestered her relentlessly for months. Finally, she gave me her permission. I called the number on Simon's card and told him I was good to go. He had a job for me right away: he was styling an advertorial for Pepe Jeans that Nick Knight was shooting. Nick was still an up-and-coming photographer, working a lot for *i-D* but also catching some early breaks shooting advertising for corporate clients, which is where the money is in fashion image-making.

(The not-so-secret secret of most independent fashion magazines is that as part of communicating their own artistic imprimatur, they function like business cards, showcasing talent which is then hired by big companies to create advertising images for proper money. Indie magazines like *i-D* and *Egoïste* in Paris, and later *Purple* and *Ten*, are crucibles of cool that the commercial world covets like crazy. The journalists moonlight writing ad and marketing copy and giving strategy advice, and the stylists and photographers create the pictures. At some point almost everyone with a fashion-media job consults for an advertiser in some way or another. If you've ever wondered why fashion news tends to be a little less adversarial than, say, politics, there's one big reason.)

Nick's wife Charlotte, mother of their three children, who also worked as Nick's shoot producer, picked me up at Richmond Station out near Kew Gardens, all the way out west, where London meets Surrey, and took me out to their house, a sort of 1950s-looking open-plan bungalow with a big garden. Charlotte was friendly and funny, but I was terrified. And I was thrilled. There I was, sixteen, on a grown-up, professional fashion shoot with an internal monologue on warp speed. *They wanted me here, but can I perform? Will anyone ask me to do something that makes me uncomfortable? Will they yell at me if they don't like what I do?* Even if I was panicking inside, I knew I was an important cog in the larger machine, and I knew not to overstep. Grace and Crosby Enninful's son was going to be polite, on time, listen, learn and do his best.

When I arrived at the house, Simon gave me a warm welcome and showed me the clothes: jeans (surprise, surprise). He told me I was to imagine that I was a character, like in a film, and explained the mood and motivation he was going for (languid, dreamy). I was to pose shirtless, which was fine with me. I was skinny as a rail at the time.

I found that I could follow Nick's directions easily, and that my shyness wasn't as big of a problem once I stepped in front of the camera. It took a few hours for me to feel my feet touch the ground, which they did on the springy green grass of Nick's backyard, where I'd go in between takes to lean up against a tree and just soak it all in. I remember the feeling of the ants from the tree crawling all over me, tickling my skin, as I thought to myself, *I like this. This is creative, this is exciting, this is happening now.* I felt myself as part of a team, there to make a moment, to capture some magic. Then I'd hear Nick's low baritone saying, 'Let's get Edward,' and I'd come trotting back in to change into more jeans and pose some more.

Nobody yelled. Nobody got angry or demanding or shitty. There were no diva fits. I'd go on to witness plenty of those, but never with Simon. There was a lot of downtime, and people told dumb jokes or gossiped about who they'd seen out at a club. They seemed happy to be together, even if once the lights turned on, everyone got serious fast. At the end of the day, we left knowing it was a job well done, and I felt like, for the first time in my life, I had found a world that made sense to me. A world that felt like mine. Or could become mine.

All my curiosity and energy now had a new outlet. I wasn't just consuming fashion magazines and defining my taste, I was actually now a participant. I told Rowan, and also Luther and Michael, all about it. Soon at school people would whisper about me when I was around. 'Oh, there's the model.' The model! I went from dorky immigrant to interesting and exotic. Yet another example of the power of fashion.

Male models have never made the same kind of money as women, and this was still a few years before the supermodels really exploded, so I never expected I'd earn a big living posing for pictures. But that afternoon at Nick's was so clarifying. I had seen what it took to make a fashion image, and it was something I could understand and participate in. It was finally demystified. I knew, no matter what, that I wanted to be in this business. This was it. As eager as I'd been to learn about music and pop stars and literature and politics and history, I was triply eager to learn about designers and clothes. Not just what labels or looks I liked. Now that I was getting a glimpse of what went on behind the entire engine of communicating about fashion, I wanted to know more. Maybe it was Simon's seriousness and precision with clothes that reminded me of my mother. Or my own childhood drawings of ladies sparking back to life in some neural pathway or other. I've always been curious and wanted to understand how things work if they interested me. This did more than interest me. I wanted to get in more deeply than just standing in front of the camera. I wanted to know what made this whole industry tick. Plus, I couldn't think of anything more inspiring. At first, though, I just kept my mouth shut and opened my eyes and ears.

There was another shoot at Nick's house, not long after the first one, this time on video. I remember walking up and down the stairs over and over. By now I was starting to feel a little bit more like myself. Simon and I had such an easy repartee, and he was always looking for new faces, so I started bringing Luther and my cousins along, and Simon would dress them up and throw them into shoots too. Luther would volunteer to DJ and keep the mood high – everybody always loved having him around.

If there was a hard part about modelling, other than me ultimately not being quite expressive nor elastic enough to be any good at it, it was the rejections. Simon cast me a lot, along with another Black kid who hung around Ladbroke Grove, Steve McQueen. (Steve would go on to win Oscars and direct some of the greatest films of our time, but then he was just my new Ladbroke Grove friend.) I'd also go out on go-sees arranged by my booker at an agency called Dolphin. I hated go-sees. If modelling makes you think at first, *Oh, I must look good*, you soon start to feel like the ugliest person in the world. I knew I wasn't getting jobs because I was too dark and African-looking. This is an especially hard lesson for a teenager to internalise, who is criss-crossing the city for days on end to stand in rooms under the gaze of white people who find his appearance to be undesirable on sight. I remember meeting Kate Moss on another go-see where I didn't get the job and she did, and being jealous and feeling like a failure. Even as an actual waif before she turned that into a genre almost single-handedly, Kate had uncontainable energy and always commanded the room, whereas I often felt myself disappear.

I wasn't the most extroverted person in the world, but I was starting to come out of my shell as I felt more familiar with fashion spaces. Most of it was due to Simon, who was not just an important figure in the industry, but a nurturing and protective mentor. He was a natural teacher and explainer, and as he recognised my curiosity, he drew me out more. He loved Ladbroke Grove and found in me, and my pipeline to my family and friends from around the way, a kind of mini-Ladbroke Grove oracle or a sort of budding muse. He clearly liked me not just for how I looked, but what I thought and said, so I trusted Simon completely. While I knew he had a taste for Black men in his love life, there was never any untoward behaviour from him. He respected me, and found in me an extremely willing student with, he said, a good eye. Simon was a father figure I felt safe with. Realness was a big thing to him – he liked streetwise looks and attitude and felt that fashion should be an expression of its time. So as weeks turned to months, he'd ask what I thought more and more. 'No, I wouldn't wear it like that,' I'd tell him. 'More like this…' and then a cuff would be adjusted or a boot unlaced, or anything to make the look more casual and less studied. It made me feel incredibly important to have his ear. Simon was a big deal.

And I loved wearing the clothes. Oh my God, how I loved the clothes. Simon loved putting me in them too. Slowly he started to transform me, as I picked up little jobs here and there as his assistant. I shaved my head completely bald and started wearing bicycle shorts with combat boots, or little tweed jackets over Katharine Hamnett T-shirts, or leather shorts or jeans he'd bleached and shredded himself before tossing them to me. Simon would give me necklaces or bags or rings and liked to see how I put them together.

While I was always unfailingly polite, I was unquenchably curious and encouraged to ask questions. Simon was happy to explain to me how he worked – and to this day I approach jobs the same way. He told me that styling wasn't just putting nice clothes on pretty people; it was creating a narrative. He started every story with a clearly defined concept and then delineated his characters. He'd get a sense of the emotion he wanted to convey, and the attitude. For visual reference and inspiration, he'd draw from his scrapbooks filled to the brim with historical and contemporary images, doodles, plates from books of paintings. Incredible amounts of time and creative energy were spent on his research. Then he'd sketch out his characters as if he were writing a movie, understanding their inner monologue, and then and only then would he start to think about clothes. When he really got going, he was consumed by this. Even if technology today has changed how I do my research, often I catch myself getting into that sort of insane inspiration-search mode, which then takes me into that screenwriter place, and I say a silent little thank you to Simon.

In addition to our ongoing dialogue around taste and style, Simon started to ask for my help scouting. I loved sizing up people, and picking out the most interesting or unusual-looking ones who still had that modelly something: tall, good bearing, great bones, a certain way of engaging with you that could become the central point of the story you might want to tell. Simon being all about multicultural casting set my imagination free as well. Fashion was what we saw and experienced in our own lives, not the tiaras and taffeta of *Tatler* and *Vogue*. And our own lives were populated by people of all colours.

As I passed from in front of the camera to behind it more and more, the best part of assisting Simon was going to the designer showrooms and pulling looks for a shoot. I knew how important the people in the photographs were, but I always came back to the clothes and how they could communicate. He loved the avant-garde Belgian designer Walter van Beirendonck, who did voluminous tailoring in dayglo colours, with giant red crosses. We'd go to every fashion house and PR office in the *i-D* universe – which meant quirky Paul Smith and over-the-top Vivienne Westwood and the big firms like Lynne Franks (the inspiration behind Jennifer Saunders's character Edina Monsoon from *Absolutely Fabulous*), Jean Bennett and Modus, who represented multiple designers at a time. It was high-octane glamour, strobe-lit, with mannequins behind glass windows, rooms and rooms of flowers and racks and racks of magic waiting to happen. Simon and I would go through it all and select. He was the king, and I was his young prince and we were here to decide what we wanted that day for the betterment of the realm.

In my short time modelling I noticed how other stylists often worked with their assistants. They'd yell at them and berate them, and blame their insufficient selection of clothes on them. I saw one stylist push his assistant over the back of a chair. Simon was a perfectionist with high standards, but when I assisted him, he was always the beautifully mannered English gentleman. If he was displeased with something, like there wasn't enough jewellery or the looks weren't coming together or something wasn't steamed or pressed right, he'd raise a polite objection in the softest voice. He was constantly touching the clothes to make sure they hung and fit the way he wanted, and in his hands, they usually did. Under his tutelage, but also informed by years at my mother's side too, I honed my eye even more sharply for how things should look, and spotted the mistakes that other stylists made on me when I was posing for them.

Modelling, and becoming a bigger part of the *i-D* crew, gave me confidence at nightclubs, which, with Simon and my snowballing band of Luther, Michael and whichever cousins were staying at our house at the time, I was starting to frequent more and more. I had started seeing a girl I had met, a model called Ngozi. We both had shaved heads and would walk around holding hands and sometimes we'd make out. We certainly looked fantastic together, but something wasn't right. She'd want to come to my place and I'd always have the excuse that my parents were home. I felt genuine affection for her, but I was starting to realise it only went so far. Maybe I was just scared? I didn't know.

Meanwhile, because of Simon, we started going more to gay bars. Luther found gay clubs like Heaven to be the easiest place in the world to get girls' phone numbers. Another place we loved was the Wag, which wasn't so much gay as just where you had to be. It was on Wardour Street in Soho and it was eclectic, both in crowd and music: hip-hop, Northern Soul, rare groove, Afrobeat, jazz, a little bit of this, a little bit of that.

John Galliano, already a star in the UK from the strength of his first few collections, hung out there. As did Boy George and Madonna. And us, emptying out of the Kensal Road flat like a clown car.

Heaven was a central meeting place for gay men, and it had a tough door policy, so there was a sense of having arrived if you made it onto its dancefloor. The look for me at Heaven was always a white tank top with tight jeans, whether blue or dip-dyed or shredded with safety pins or custom bleached. The music was soulful house, which I could certainly dance to. The first time I ever got high on anything other than beer was at Heaven. It was microdot acid, and it made the whole room come alive with colour, sound and movement. I was with Luther and Michael that night, and Michael wasn't feeling quite the same euphoria. Michael is one of the stubbornest and most talented people in my extended family, and even then he could bring the drama. He started freaking out and Luther and I ended up having to talk him down for hours.

We were teenagers, still in school, and we weren't supposed to go out. My dad had no idea how much I was working already, or what kind of life I was really leading, though he assumed whatever it was, it was bad. He'd lock the door before he went to bed, and it was meant to stay locked. Michael and I would tiptoe out, take the bus to whichever club it was that night, dance on the podiums, drink too much, maybe drop a little something, maybe not, and come back before dawn. Sometimes we'd have coordinated with my cousins Lomo and Sasha, who stayed with us for long stretches of time, to sneak down and unlock the door at a certain hour. Once I tried throwing stones at the window, which then woke up my dad, who came to the door shouting and didn't stop for days after.

Though Michael was starting to get fairly out there with his look – the T-shirts ever tighter, the hairdos more sculpted – somehow he managed to be my father's favourite. This is the same man who told us all that if he found out we were gay he'd slit our throats, and yet Michael, the most flamboyant of us all, clearly a budding friend of Dorothy's, could do no wrong. We just laughed at my father's threats, anyway. He had been making them since well before I was born and somehow we were all still standing and breathing fresh air. One afternoon I was at the flat after school with Rowan, and he and Michael started parrying back and forth: 'You're gay!' 'No, you're gay!' Honestly, it was like that meme of the multiple Spider-Men all pointing at each other.

Meanwhile, I was starting to have crushes on men, like James Dublin, another model scouted by Simon. He was massively tall and brawny, like he was chiselled from stone, dark as me, with big pillowy lips. I was obsessed with him. He lived out east, across town in Poplar and spoke with a cockney accent. He had attitude for days and most people were awestruck and petrified. If anyone dared speak to him at Heaven, he'd just scowl. James was gay, Michael was gay, Simon was gay, Rowan was gay, and I was, I don't know: flickering?

I figured it out soon enough. I hadn't been assisting Simon for more than a year when he got a call to style a Levi's campaign in New York and asked me to come along. Simon consulted for the company a little, like a freelance creative director, working on ad campaigns and posters. He'd cast and style and do conceptual work. I was so excited to go I couldn't contain myself. If Great Britain was a big deal to a Ghanaian kid, New York was basically the moon. It was the city every kid in the world already knew from movies and TV, and now it was my turn: at age seventeen, I was going with Simon to work on a fashion shoot. This was the dream. It was springtime, and before we travelled I stayed up all night planning my outfits: denim shorts, ripped jeans, Katharine Hamnett slogan T-shirts, my cowboy boots, of course, a cotton jacket with velvet sleeves, and some short shorts, because I had heard about the Sound Factory and vogueing and I wasn't going to miss that.

I remember like it was yesterday the first time I saw the skyline driving into Manhattan from JFK Airport over the 59th Street bridge. There was a massive Calvin Klein billboard on the side of a skyscraper and I said to Simon how amazing it must be to have your work up there. My eyes were enormous and in New York, fashion was everywhere. Levi's had put us up at a low-key hotel in Midtown, which was fine with Simon, who didn't have a diva's bone in his body. We weren't there to lounge around in bathrobes anyway, but to spend two days in the client's showroom pulling clothes, and then another two days on a set in an industrial loft downtown. The cast was

New York, 2014. With Alec
and our Boston Terrier, Ru

Longleat House, 2022. Cutting
the wedding cake with Alec

Tema, Ghana, 1970s.
Grace Enninful, my mother

Ghana, 1960s. Major Crosby
Kofi Enninful, my father

Tema, Ghana, 1980. Top row, left to right: Kenneth Enninful; Joel Enninful; my father, Crosby; my mother, Grace; Luther Enninful. Below: Akua Enninful (on Crosby's lap); me; an unnamed family friend

Tamale, Ghana, mid-1960s. My mother, Grace Aboah, before she married my father, Crosby

Takoradi, Ghana, 1972.
My mother holding me

Tema, Ghana, early 1980s.
My mother, Grace, and
sister, Mina

London, mid-1990s. In front of
the family's house in the council
estate on Kensal Road. Left to
right: Akua, Mina and Grace

London, 1985. Age 13, in a
school photo from Lilian Baylis
Technology School

London, 1991. In the offices of *i-D*

London, 1991. With Michael Boadi in Michael's father's apartment in Poplar

London, 1994

London, 1992

London, 1991. Modelling
for an *i-D* story

London, 1992. Clockwise from
top left: me, stylist Lance Martin,
Philip Ofogba, Simon Foxton,
Raymond (a friend who worked
for Vivienne Westwood),
Luther, Michael, most probably
at Heaven

London, 1993. With stylist
Anna Cockburn at a fashion show

London, 1994. On set with
Eugene Souleiman

New York City, 1994. Kate
Moss and Naomi Campbell
on *i-D*'s August 1994 cover

New York City, 1994. Naomi
and Kate for *i-D*. This photo was
often used for the 'You Can't Sit
With Us' meme

London, 1993. With Craig and
Pat on set at Metro Studios

New York City, 1996. Polaroid
of Kate Moss in one of Craig
McDean's campaigns for
CK Khakis

New York City, 1996. Kate
Moss and a male model for
CK Khakis

big and diverse, with men and women, so we had a lot to get organised and prepared. The Polaroid camera never stopped spitting out test looks that we'd lay out in a grid on a big table and pore over like archaeologists, analysing, judging, tweaking.

But the real fun was at night after Simon went to bed. The second night we were in town was a Friday, so I put on my hot pants and cowboy boots and headed down to 27th Street to Sound Factory, all by myself. I must have looked cute because I cleared the door immediately and was swallowed up into that notorious wonderland. There were drag queens touching up their makeup in the bathrooms, and gorgeous women enlaced in the arms of gorgeous men, and house music throbbing throughout the small rooms upstairs and the cavernous dancefloor downstairs, where bodies writhed under a giant disco ball. I stayed for hours and hours, wandering from room to room, dancing, checking people out. The vogueing finally started happening at four in the morning.

The crowd had thinned out by then, and as I scanned it, I saw a gorgeous blond across the room. He was older, maybe in his thirties, with buzzed hair and blue eyes. I had only had crushes on Black men; this was the first time a white man really caught my eye. So what was I going to do about it? I said to myself, *OK, Edward, you are living the life you always wanted. This is your time. You are feeling yourself. There's nobody here you know. You're free. Get on with it.*

I crossed the room, my heart pounding out of my chest. I said hello and before I knew it, the guy grabbed me and we started making out. It was the most thrilling feeling of all, in a period of months where it seemed like I had nothing but thrilling feelings. If I had been edging around the question of my sexual orientation, now there was no more question. Fireworks went off inside me, the whole thing. Just as I had found myself in fashion, which was what I wanted to do in the world, now I was discovering more intimate terrain. I felt free. And scared. And excited. I was shot through with pure joy. It was about time.

The next morning, on next-to-no sleep – because what even was sleep? – Simon asked me why I couldn't stop smiling. To this day I never told him why. Simon was a father figure to me and though he went out, he didn't stay out, and he didn't approve of too much clubbing. But I couldn't stop smiling because the pieces of my life were falling into place, fast, in ways I hadn't ever dared to dream.

I had a newfound confidence when we got back to London, where I was making a home for myself at *i-D*. I spent practically all of my time away from school at the office in Shoreditch, which was very much under the influence of Terry Jones's wife Tricia. Tricia's edict was to leave bitchiness at the door. Well aware of the tendency of young fashionistas to let their attitudes run away with them, she used to lecture the receptionists to be nice to everyone. No divas allowed. Her feeling was, it's intimidating to young photographers and models to come here, so be kind and welcoming. Terry was out of town a lot, first for Fiorucci and then eventually for

Esprit, where he became creative director. The big-money gigs like that helped keep the lights on at *i-D*, which at this point was half owned by *Time Out*. Tricia still came around a lot, with cakes and cookies, to make sure we were eating.

What was the point of food, anyway? Cigarettes and whatever I'd grab on the run were fine for me. If I wasn't assisting Simon, I was starting to write about fashion news for Beth Summers, who was the overall fashion editor, and coordinated the whole department, including womenswear, and written content. Beth was terrifying to most people – not only was she always dressed in black with combat boots and fingers full of rings, she was direct as hell. She said it like she saw it and had zero time for fakers and idiots. She went to Central Saint Martins with Simon, whom she loved, and was sharp and intelligent. I, who have always found myself like a purring kitten in the company of fierce women, loved her immediately. She never gave me any grief, never condescended, and always encouraged me.

Beth shared Simon's and my obsession with realness, which was starting to coalesce into a style people would eventually call 'grunge'. Like Simon, Beth also encouraged me to style, and pointed out some of the really young photographers who were starting to show their books to Terry, like a kid called Craig McDean. We were an up-and-coming generation, she said, and we should have our turn to make our mark. I loved styling, but I wasn't comfortable enough with my own ambition to imagine I could become a stylist myself, even if Simon and

I brainstormed a lot. But as I was always good in my literature studies, I was comfortable writing, so I hovered around Beth's desk and picked up shopping pages and little newsy blurbs. Anything she asked me to do would be done, to my very best, right away. She thought I was funny and encouraged me to lean into that as a writer, so I developed a chatty, sort-of punchy style on the page.

A few months after my trip to New York, Fashion Week was happening in Paris, and Terry decided to send me to cover it. The magazine would pay for my ticket over, and gave me the mandate that I didn't need to see every show, just the sort of avant-garde ones that were important to our audience: John Galliano, Helmut Lang, Martin Margiela, Yohji Yamamoto, Jean Colonna, Jean-Paul Gaultier, Vivienne Westwood and my favourite, Rei Kawakubo's Comme des Garçons.

It was the latter, back in London on an early visit with Simon, that first made me see women's fashion in a new way. We went to the Comme showroom in Holland Park to look at menswear for a shoot. I spied a crazy black dress out of the corner of my eye and fell in love. It was asymmetrical and had odd pleats, and was a bit askew and so intelligent. I looked through the rest of the women's racks and was amazed by the different silhouettes and textures, and how there was always a much larger idea than just being pretty or flattering. It was such a different point of view, and always meant to communicate something else. So I was very excited to get to attend their show, even if, like just about everywhere that season, I would end up either in a nosebleed seat, or in standing room with the fashion students.

This was my first trip alone, and I was still technically underage. Before I left for the airport, Terry told me, 'Just be yourself and write what you see.' Then Simon took me aside and gave me more detailed instructions: I was to take the bus from Charles de Gaulle Airport to Charles de Gaulle Étoile, and then catch a metro from there to Madeleine, where he assured me I could find an inexpensive hotel. He knew I had no money of my own, so he pressed £200 into my hand, out of his own pocket. I did what he said and went to a dumpy little place on the rue Tronchet. There wasn't enough money for the whole trip, but I could at least get my bearings somewhere central.

Even if no one knew who I was in the show tents, and I had the worst seats in the house, I didn't care. My distance from the catwalk made the whole thing feel even more theatrical and spectacular. Everyone should watch a show from the standing section at least once in their lives. You're surrounded by students, craning their necks for a view. Even if you're the most jaded fashionista in the world, their excitement is contagious. I remember Galliano's collection of spaghetti-strap slip dresses and low-slung trousers topped with vests and blouses with exaggerated flouncy bows, and a whole cache of shredded white outerwear that made the models look like clouds. So many ideas, so many motifs. Martin Margiela's casting blew my mind. He was the first designer to put waify grunge models on the catwalk – Kate

Moss was still only just breaking out internationally – and in their little T-shirts and necklaces, they looked like a bunch of Ladbroke Grove girls to me.

In addition to the shows, I went to showroom appointments at press offices like Michèle Montagne, who had really cool designers. Even if I was totally anonymous at the shows, she welcomed me like an old friend and made me feel at home. All the PRs did. They loved *i-D*. But outside fashion's cocoon, it was another story. One afternoon I had gone to the Comme des Garçons office for the first time, the seat of their creative operations outside Tokyo, and it was like going to church. Rei Kawakubo is famously shy but her team has always been down to earth and eminently relatable. Afterwards, I was feeling so happy on place Vendôme on a beautiful afternoon, when two police officers stopped me and asked me for my papers. I went from a dauphin to a street rat in a split-second. Bubble burst. Looking around me, I saw I was the only person on the whole open square, opposite the Ritz and surrounded by glittering jewellery shops, who got that treatment. I was also, I noticed as I pulled out my passport, the only Black person around. What a coincidence.

But place Vendôme wasn't the only address that mattered in Paris, which is one of the most multicultural cities in Europe. After the shows, I'd go to Barbès-Rochechouart, still a very African district today, for Senegalese food with André Walker, a Black American designer, and my friend Angie Rubini, another Black American who was working in the

PR department at Comme. We'd talk shit and make fun of all the uptight people and designers we thought were too over the top and 80s.

After Simon's cash ran out, I slept on the couch in the apartment of my friend Mike McKay, a model from Manchester whom I knew from castings in London. He had a tiny, tiny place with a super-high ceiling in the very north of the city. After the shows, we'd talk and smoke packs of cigarettes till it was time to go out to Le Queen or Les Bains Douches, or wherever the party was that night. Perhaps this little routine was why Mike's girlfriend was not thrilled by my presence. Mike told me he had had it with modelling and wanted to open a club. After Mike's couch was no longer an option, I got in touch with one of my aunties, who was living in a little apartment in the western suburb of Saint-Cloud. The first night I was meant to stay there, I showed up at five in the morning after a night out at I can't remember where. And so my first night there was also my last. Thankfully, I was due to return home soon.

When I look back at what I wrote that season, in my infinite teenage wisdom, I die inside just a little. 'I'd like to be able to say that Jean-Paul Gaultier was a hit. I'd like to, but I can't...' Terry told me after I filed my copy that I might want to tone down the acidity just a wee bit. Fair enough. I was flailing around, and maybe trying too hard. But writing wasn't as thrilling to me as image-making. In writing about fashion, you're at a distance. You assess what a designer does, and give it context, but you're not contributing to the process itself.

This may have brought out my young urge to draw too thick a line under everything in writing. Not everything needed an exclamation point. Not everything had to be a manifesto.

Styling and photography, to me, offered a more interesting seat at the table, even if taking that seat still intimidated the hell out of me. (This is sometimes how the most tightly held dreams are – you need a little time to warm up to where you can finally dare.) In creating fashion stories, you're adding your own interpretation and spin to what designers have done. You're inserting yourself much more into the conversation and adding your own layer on top. Stylists work hand in hand with designers in a way that writers do not. That creativity moves in a different way. It's more instinctual for me, and honestly more fun. It's also a massive delegation and managing operation, being in charge of ten spinning plates at once, coordinating with the photographer, hair and makeup, coaching the model, coming up with the concept. I was dying to start doing it, but I wasn't going to be too pushy.

It took Simon and Beth's encouragement to put myself out there more. But they weren't just going to give me a story to do, so first I had to organise test shoots. With their help getting PR people to lend clothes to me, I set up my first with Luther as the model and Michael doing the hair, shot by a friend of mine from school called Padraig. We went out to his house in East London in a strange postwar development we called Toy Town, because of its attempt to do brutalist picturesque, with little bridges connecting the buildings.

The vibe of my shoot was basically butch Black gay realness, a watered-down version of what Simon had already perfected. We had a few drinks and then I got very serious and gave Luther all his poses. 'Stand here, put your hand on your waist.' It was awkward and studied. Simon was encouraging of the results, but I knew men's fashion wasn't where it was at for me.

The really fantastical work was happening with women's fashion, which was a much better outlet for my ongoing obsession with women and their style, in all their infinite and inspirational guises. It was also a much more competitive field. Simon once again gave me the push I needed, telling me to call his photographer friend Peter Ward, and offering his help to ask all the press offices to lend me the clothes. We shot black and white around the South Bank – more concrete, more urban realism – on a few moody-looking Black girls, including one called Fina, who ended up getting pretty big for a minute.

My impulse was to show my reality, only a heightened version of it. The girls were all in tight ski pants and big jackets, badly done minimalism. I was trying to recreate what I learned from Simon, but just put it on women, so it was a very obvious and schematic programme: each look was a men's item paired with a women's item. Styling, I would learn later, is one of those things that you get better at over time, as you learn visual shortcuts. Looking at that story now, I could have made the whole narrative point with just a haircut, or some lipstick on a boy. I didn't need the men's shoe and the men's jacket over the dress. But I was a desperately enthusiastic kid with a pressing need to express myself, and I still had everything to learn.

The point of all the tests was to show them to Terry and see if he'd run them. He didn't, but they were enough to get a commission from him, as long as Simon agreed to help. It was a story called Pan-Global, in which I put a diverse cast of models in switched-up national costume. A very blonde girl in African gear, a Black girl in something cowboy. With all the mixing and symbolism, it was maybe my own ham-fisted attempt at Buffalo, although I hadn't really made the connection. It's another somewhat painful one to look at today, though I can't fault myself for the multicultural impulse. It's one of the things that brought me here, after all.

Still, I must have been doing something right, since Beth then commissioned me to style a story with the photographer Jason Evans, whom I still modelled for occasionally. It was more gorgeous Black girls, this time going about their business: reading books, going out for drinks, lots of daily-life scenes, but in clothes that I had shredded and customised myself. That process took months, and I did it at the office and even a little bit at home, far from my father's watchful eyes. *i-D* was a monthly, without a website that needed to be updated minute to minute with its own insatiable demand for images. Back then we could assemble a single story over weeks, finding the clothes, getting one look shot, coming back, developing it, then going out and shooting another. I still love that story, with those thoughtful, studious girls. It's the one where I see best the seeds of what I became.

By then I had just started to develop a way of working that I've since come to rely on absolutely. After all the conceptual work defining the characters in the shoot, as Simon taught me, it would only be when I went to sleep that everything finally crystallised. It's like I'd watch the shoot in my sleep, wake up in the morning, and, if the concept was working, I'd have every single image in the story: what the girls would be wearing, the set, hair, makeup, the nails, the brow, all of it. If everything wasn't visualised by the time I woke up, I knew I still needed to pinpoint the concept some more because something was still not all there.

Even though it was a reliable way of working, I used to think this kind of productive dreaming was cheating. Maybe because Black people have always been told we must work twice as hard, and ease in labour isn't a concept usually reserved for us, but I thought having something just come to me easily and automatically made me an impostor. Then years later, someone finally told me, no, it's a gift. Whatever it is, it's become my process, it involves my unconscious mind and I've learned to trust it.

By this point, I'd finished Kingsway College and needed to find a university 'so I could study law', as my father would have wanted. Pfft. I had no interest in further study whatsoever, but that wasn't going to cut it in Crosby Enninful's house. Steve McQueen, my fellow model with a monster brain and insatiable intellectual curiosity, told me he was going to Goldsmiths. You could often find Steve and me on Old Compton Street in Soho, at some café or other, drinking endless cups of coffee, running a commentary on the outfits parading past us. (Even now I can still make Steve laugh with a cock of the head and a well-timed, 'Look at *her.*') If Goldsmiths was good enough for Steve, I thought, well then that's where I'll go too. It was a competitive school with a strong reputation in the humanities, which was technically what I liked best. I applied, and since I had always had good marks, I got in.

The problem was, then I had to go to class. On the first day of school, I walked up with Steve to the door of some lecture hall or other. The door opened, I took one look inside, told him, 'Man, I can't do this', and bolted. Steve still tells that story like it was the only day I ever set foot on campus.

The truth was my quitting school was a little more gradual than that. One day, after a string of notable absences, one of my Goldsmiths tutors, a kindly English teacher who taught Jane Austen, asked me point blank, 'What are you doing here?' She wasn't being hostile; what she meant was, you know what you want to do with your life already and you're doing it. You're in a position most of your fellow students wouldn't even dare to dream of being in. Why are you bothering with us? You don't need this. It reminded me of my mother, essentially getting turned away from technical college in Accra because she was already so firmly on her path.

She gave me the permission I needed to stop going to class at all. There was just one problem: my father. For months I kept up a sad charade of leaving the house in the morning 'in time for class', when all the while I was going to showroom appointments, in and out of the offices of *i-D*, and to photoshoots. He had no idea. He'd ask me how school was going, and I'd lie and lie and feel horrible about it.

Finally, I couldn't take it any more. One morning I was due in to the *i-D* offices to meet with Beth and I ran into my father. He asked me, once again, how my studies were. I told him I hadn't been going to school, but that I'd been working at *i-D*, and I'd found what I wanted to do with my life. I thought of the words of my tutor and how encouraging she was. Maybe my father would see it like her?

Not so much. He flew into a savage rage, made a beeline for my bedroom, and started throwing my things out of the window. My precious clothes, shoes, cowboy boots, my life in fact, things that meant so much to me and had come to represent who I was and how I thought of myself and what I wanted to show the world. All of it went out the window. I was lucky I wasn't next, though my father told me I would no longer be welcome in the house. My mother was downstairs in her workroom the whole time, the sound of her machine drowning out half the noise. (The other half wouldn't have even raised her eyebrow – my father yelled all the time.) There was nothing I could do, nor did I want to. I had had it with his lectures and bullshit. I was pursuing a dream, encouraged by successful and even sometimes moderately responsible adults. Fuck this, I thought. I'm out of here, and walked out the door.

Still in shock, I did the only thing I knew how to do: I went to work. I headed into the office, completely shaken, and went to see Beth. She would surely have some advice, or an idea, or even just some kind words. I was still trembling when I knocked on her door. But before I could even tell her what had just happened, she told me she was leaving the magazine, and it had been decided with Terry that I was going to take her place. I was eighteen.

GRUNGE

London, 1993. At my desk at i-D's Covent Garden office.
Smoking is bad for your health.

CHAPTER FOUR

I imagine that I had a huge smile on my face as I thanked Beth profusely upon hearing the news, but inwardly, I was spent. Between getting kicked out of home and this surreal offer, it was a lot for one day, and it wasn't even lunchtime.

After letting it sink in for a moment, and going to say thank you to Terry, I went back to my parents' place to gather up my things. By 'gather', I mean that I stood in the street and retrieved the remnants of my young life from the courtyard outside the family home, where they lay lifeless, like dead bodies, macabre. *I have somewhere else to be, somewhere better*, I told myself, rescuing tank tops, acid-wash jeans and cowboy boots and cramming them into a plastic bin bag. *Some of these clothes will need to be washed now,* I sighed. *That man has no idea what they mean to me.*

After a lifetime of my father's tyranny, I was done. My mother later told me over the phone, when I called to check in, that she was sure my father didn't mean it. She was clearly sad, but reverted to type, saying that's just how he is, so why was I being so dramatic about it? Dramatic or not, I was drawing a firm line. This was my life; it was no longer a question of bending to my father's will. Like my mother, Luther and Kenneth assumed it was just another bad fight and that I'd be back, but my feeling as I looked up at the window while scraping my stuff up off the ground was: *Good riddance. I'm never coming back.* Michael's father had a small flat on a council estate in Poplar. He was a devout Christian and not much fun, but he was also back in Ghana, so the place was empty for a few months at least. Michael proposed that we crash there. 'If you're out of there, I'm out,' he said of the flat where he spent most of his time. 'Let's go.'

I was in terrible shock. It was the second time in seven years that I had been ejected from the only home I knew, and this time it was worse, because I was being separated from my family. Even if that was the point – to get away from my father's oppressive bullshit – it was incredibly disorienting for someone like me, who was hardly ever far from them, and, consequentially, also hardly ever alone. I stuffed the chaos down by focusing all my efforts on the magazine and the new life that so suddenly came with it. I had a lot of catching up to do. At eighteen, I had just become the youngest person at any international fashion publication to hold the position of fashion director – the record still probably stands to this day.

I was green, but I had a lot of opinions and ideas, and I was comfortable enough talking to Terry, even if my work had mostly passed through intermediaries like Beth and Simon.

But my God, the job was massive. I'd be wrangling musicians, models, aristocrats and what we called 'real people' – meaning interesting civilians – to fill the magazine's pages. I was also commissioning the photographers who would shoot them, and often styling the shoots myself. I would be commissioning other photographers and stylists to do fashion stories for 'the well', the section of the magazine towards the back where these spreads lived. Also, importantly, I'd be responsible for filling the shopping and news pages in the front section, writing the copy and ensuring that the designers and shops featured were always '*i-D*'. And I'd have to get it all past Terry, and our editor-in-chief Matthew Colin, as well as Nick Knight, who was now our consulting photo editor and an important conduit to new, young talent.

This job was as much about politics as it was about writing, assisting or simply styling, and I was a baby. I'd have to act with authority, making creative decisions for the magazine and executing them, corralling people across departments like design and layout, advertising and marketing. I'd have to say no to top stylists and photographers whose work I admired. There was a culture of permissiveness and creativity around *i-D*. Terry would give photographers creative freedom, but he could also be tough on them, and when he was out of town, as he often was, I'd have to carry out his mandates with stalwarts whose long and illustrious careers preceded my time there. Imagine eighteen-year-old me calling you up to explain we'd taken another look at your story, and that image you were madly keen on sadly isn't going to make the cut? Some days I couldn't believe I got away with it myself. But then, as now, my advice is this: whether the news you have to impart is good, bad or simply awkward, tell it fast, tell it kindly and move on. It's not personal.

Because *i-D* bred such loyalty and offered so much creative freedom, people didn't leave, even when they broke out to more lucrative, mainstream pastures. Judy Blame might have been styling Boy George and Neneh Cherry and had Björk buzzing around him, but he was also still contributing regularly to *i-D*, and I'd be one of the people deciding how to work with him. Simon was a bit wary of Judy – they were rivals in some ways. Where Simon was grounded, Judy, as I observed from seeing him around the office, and even before, as a model on a few of his shoots, was hedonistic and tart, with out-there ideas. They were both geniuses when it came to work.

Even if I was panicking some days, every self-critical voice inside me chattering nonstop, I can see now how I was propelled by ambition. At any given hour, on any given project, I couldn't wait to dive in. Alongside all the life tumult and heady living, daily deadlines would keep me in the office late at night. That was fine with me. I had the manic energy of someone who had just lost his family and was desperate to create a new one. Rushing into this world of noise and new people and constant activity and deadlines was a way to tune out the fear, but also to recreate the hectic ambience I had just given up, even if the value system and customs of this new place were completely different.

There was no off switch when it came to my life at *i-D*. In the after hours, together with my fellow editors, I was supposed to represent the magazine to the world at large. We put on roving *i-D* nights in clubs across the country that I'd be expected to attend and promote in our pages. From Manchester to Liverpool, Glasgow to Cardiff, venues would pay to get us and our DJs and friends out there on hired coaches to bring a bit of London to the rest of the country. Luther would usually come along, as would young *i-D* photographers like Wolfgang Tillmans and Juergen Teller. Juergen's surreal, surprising, sometimes deer-in-the-headlights style was honed at *i-D*, where cheekiness and confrontation were part of our identity. Sometimes I'd be so busy that when the arm of my glasses broke, I'd just wrap them around my ear with thread and keep going, even if the thread cut the delicate skin behind my ear and made it bleed. Dab it away and get on with it.

I learned to circulate at nights like these – to move through a crowd, say hello and make small talk, while inwardly ordering myself not to put a foot wrong. I started developing a protective shell to manage the internal disconnect. Once my guard was up, I liked representing the magazine, and found that with the increased legitimacy of my position, I could talk to people more easily. I could be the life of the party now, but a piece of me was always elsewhere, sorting through what I had to do the next day. My courage was fuelled by drink, adrenaline and the armour I was styling myself in. I had started to dress like a proper fashion director. Think lots of black and white, stiff Helmut Lang jeans, and little shrunken V-neck sweaters over starched shirts topped off with a big camel Crombie. On point, but never too wild, lest I come off as a fashion victim. We editors needed to stand back just a bit, and so our look was chic, but restrained.

i-D's HQ at the time was on Curtain Road in Shoreditch. Back then the neighbourhood was almost unrecognisable from the moneyed approximation of cool it would later become. The warehouse buildings that are now Shoreditch House and the Boundary Hotel were derelict factories. We may have been there, but it was not the ground zero of anything. Walking the deserted cobbled streets to and from the nearby pubs, the occasional random creep poking out of an alley, was dodgy at times. A few months later, *i-D* would move to a different set of cobbled streets in Covent Garden, close to Seven Dials and a stiletto's throw from Soho. That was a bit more fun.

My new desk was opposite Paul Hunwick, the production manager, and an operations hub. Art and photography books were stacked everywhere, with print schedules sellotaped up to what free wall space we had left. The office had bare lightbulbs hanging from the ceiling and whitewashed walls. It was not outwardly glamorous, but it was buzzing.

Paul was Beth's best friend, and he was going to keep an eye on me, so of course the first thing he did once it got dark after my first full day of work was offer me a drag off a spliff. I might have been from Ladbroke Grove, but no matter how many nightclubs I had been to and no matter how many joints my brothers smoked, I still hadn't tried that particular substance. The paranoia hit the moment I inhaled. I somehow made it to the train and back to Michael's father's flat, despite being sure that everyone around me was about to have me arrested. Everything was already new and strange. Now it was even stranger.

Michael's dad's tiny two-bedroom council flat was basically empty except for stacks of rectangular, zip-top woven plastic shopping bags stuffed with his belongings, a little like how we stacked our suitcases back in Accra. Everyone called them 'Ghana Must Go bags', so named for a 1980s expulsion of undocumented Ghanaians from Nigeria, who had to pack up everything they owned in them. (Those bags are iconic and used by immigrants all over; Balenciaga put out a woven leather version in 2017.)

The building was red brick, with balconies wrapped around the outside of the flats, in a neighbourhood mostly filled with post-war concrete. It stood in the shadow of the Balfron Tower, today considered a sort of brutalist masterpiece that hadn't yet aged into being aesthetically interesting. The three months Michael and I spent in that flat before his father came home were a gleeful liberation for us both. There was no one to avoid, no reason to sneak around, no one to yell at us. Not a crumb of food was cooked in that apartment, nor a bed made. We'd drink cans of Red Stripe beer and then go clubbing, with a steady stream of people coming back home with us afterwards. It was a revolving door of friends and beautiful strangers, dirty ashtrays and empties and takeout boxes. I remember dry-shaving my head bald in the bathroom before going out to Heaven, Michael and Rowan watching me in the mirror as the hair landed softly in the sink.

I was still chaste, pretty much just kissing boys – perhaps a little light cuddling if I was feeling especially wild – and wishing for a Prince Charming. For a different person at a different time in history, this forward career motion, with its attendant ego boost, might have caused an explosion of libido. But I was terrified of sex. This wasn't the healthiest place to be emotionally, although I thank God to this day for my prudery, because the AIDS crisis was raging. People I knew from Ladbroke Grove and the clubs were vanishing as the Grim Reaper hacked his way through London. There was a menacing ad on TV, with haunting music by Brian Eno, showing an iceberg breaking to pieces: 'There is now a deadly virus. . . So far it has been confined to small groups,' read the spare-looking copy, referring to me and my new tribe, 'but it's spreading. And unless we act now, it's going to get much, much worse.' There was so much fear, so much vulnerability in this community that I had just become a part of. Even if I did badly want someone to call my own, I only had a child's idea of what that even meant.

When you grow up gay in a world primed to detest you, you often have to grow up twice. Once when you leave home, where more often than not, it was your being gay that made you leave. And then a second time when you find the gay community and discover a whole new set of rules and codes to switch in and out of. With those rules came a whole new set of potential rejections, too.

Now add to that being Black and an immigrant, and working class. The gay culture of 1990s Britain wasn't so much coded in its racism as flat-out racist. I mixed it up in clubs, and I liked all different kinds of men, especially working-class ones like me. But I noticed that among some white gay men there were terms and obvious fetishes that made me feel categorised and objectified and pissed off. I wasn't about to be a plaything in someone else's drama. I would be the star of my own. White men who preferred Black men were called 'dinge queens', as if we were dirty or dingy. White men who liked East Asian men were called 'rice queens', 'curry queens' for South Asians and so on. What an infuriating and toxic idea. If I met a white man out at night who was known on the whisper circuit to date only Black men, it was another reason, and a good one, to keep my distance. It's advice I'd give to any gay man of colour today, as racism still poisons gay spaces, even if it's more euphemistic and slippery. As ugly as my experience was, overt racism was easier to suss out than the more polite prejudice of today. It breaks my heart that the safe space that all young people deserve to have continues to be such a poisoned well for people of colour.

Confused and overwhelmed, I held myself apart from others. Once again, work – obsessive, breathless, important, exciting work – was there to take me away from anything messy and help me hide away from matters of the heart. I dated a bit, but boyfriends were still a fantasy. Out of circumstance, immaturity and self-preservation, I was untouchable. All I knew at the time was that I wanted to be well dressed, to laugh, and make beautiful, interesting, meaningful pictures. We were all so good at burning the candle at both ends at *i-D*, and coming from an African family as I did, where your work is so connected to your self-worth, it seemed normal to me that this new life I was building revolved entirely around the job.

I always had a template for hard work in my mother. Though I was by now at arm's length from my family, I felt a piece of her spirit in me whenever I focused on the task in hand. I had got into the habit of calling her from time to time to check in. To make things easy, I'd try to time it for when I knew my father wouldn't be home. 'I miss you,' she would tell me, shattering my heart for a moment. Then I'd harden my shell a little more, as I threw myself into another eighteen-hour work day.

I felt so rejected by my family, and so eager to find my own space in the world, that, defensively, I rejected them right back. I reached out less, and opened up less when I did reach out. I have a lot of queer friends who have been through this: stung by our families' misunderstanding and judgement, we shut ourselves down emotionally when we're around them, even if perhaps we could have arrived at a deeper understanding with a little more conversation. Not that it's only on the kids to build that bridge – it should be adult work, by any logic – but I miss my mother so much now and I know that because of my father's rejection, and how I defended myself against it, I lost time with her before she died. Everyone in my family is proud, including me. It's a great quality until it isn't.

As I started to get into a rhythm at *i-D*, I was able to keep the focus up, hit every deadline, take every call and every meeting, but it never ended. Since we partied with the same people we spent all day with, either in the office, on set or at the clubs, everything sort of folded together. Whether in the middle of a nightclub or walking down Portobello or sitting in the pub, some fashion conversation was being had, or the look of some girl or boy across the room was being noted down for inspiration for a shoot.

I looked the part and, to the outside world, anointed as I was as *i-D*'s fashion director, I was becoming known, recognised by people I didn't already know, and sought out. But I suffered such a massive case of impostor syndrome. How could I not, given how quickly everything had come together? And impostor syndrome is something every Black person has been conditioned to feel. It's the energy of, 'What are you doing here?' internalised into a kind of constant feedback loop. Very soon after I started, I had a meeting with David Sims, who was the hot photographer in our London world, an alt-culture Superman. Handsome and smart, he was everyone's crush, and I had to talk ideas with him as if it were no big deal. *i-D*'s office may have relocated to the Seven Dials Warehouse in slightly chicer Covent Garden, but the interior was as *derelicte* as the previous digs. At lunch next door, as David was talking about an upcoming shoot he wanted to do – likely a grungy, yet sensitive concept – I was having a parallel internal conversation with myself: *OK, you have to be someone else now. You have to be a grown-up; no more being a kid.*

I told myself to treat this adult me as a new persona. Immigrants are experts at code-switching, gay immigrants exponentially so, and this would be no different from that, as long as I could hold it together. Which I did, though it came at a price. With the authority bestowed upon me by my job, my shyness ended up being interpreted as a frostiness that took years to melt off my reputation. French art director Roland Mouret — later to become a prominent designer — told me he used to hate coming into the office for our scheduled appointments, because I seemed so quiet and imperious. If only he knew that I felt like I was dangling on a ledge above the abyss of chaos.

Despite my generally introverted demeanour, I had a hell of a lot to do, and my desk became a waystation for visiting photographers and musicians and models and, importantly, other stylists. Cathy Kasterine, well regarded for bringing an updated, hippy, nebulous, flower-power aesthetic to Corinne Day's shoots, minimalist queen Melanie Ward, who worked a lot with Corinne too, and Venetia Scott, a frequent collaborator of Juergen's, who had a flair for English eccentricity, would all come around and pitch ideas. I wanted their contributions recognised, so I also wrote profiles of them for the magazine and set up monthly meetings where we could all come together and discuss story ideas.

Stylists are more reliable generators of ideas than photographers, anyway. This is not to belittle the contribution of photographers — it's just that stylists often think in broad narrative concepts, and of course we are focused on clothes, when some photographers can be more focused on image treatment and mood and technique. These are equally important, but not always the first order of business when planning pages. And since I was responsible for the entire fashion output of the magazine, not just styling my own shoots, I couldn't indulge in competitiveness with my peers. We needed everybody's contribution to put out a good issue.

By the time I got my job, Michael had been climbing his own ladder. He had no beauty-school training and just a little time working in salons, but his talent was monstrous, and people recognised it quickly. He started shooting a lot with Mark Lebon, who worked out of his studio/crash pad called Crunch, a scruffy, two-storey converted garage on Wakeman Road. I already knew who Mark was from seeing him around Ladbroke Grove as a kid, a big teddy bear with a booming voice, wearing Christopher Nemeth vegetable-dyed ragamuffin suits. He was a kind of Ladbroke Grove Buddhist sage, who opened his doors to collaborators and friends, many of them young kids he'd end up mentoring. Kate Moss lived in his flat on Kensal Road, across the street from my family, when she first came north from Croydon, after showing up at Crunch for a go-see, still in her school uniform.

As well as Mark, Kate had been working frequently with Corinne Day, who bounced back and forth between *i-D* and *The Face*, and who was a crucial part of this new, stripped-down, naturalistic mood that was arising, of which Kate was fast becoming the muse.

Kate was at Crunch a lot, which made sense even if she wasn't working with Mark nonstop, because Kate has always been wherever the best party is. Crunch's ground floor was like a West London version of Andy Warhol's Factory. Hammocks were strewn around, and a big bed functioned as a conference table. Mark was the epicentre of a loose arts collective that he and Judy Blame belonged to called the House of Beauty and Culture that, along with Christopher Nemeth and the proto-steampunk shoe designer John Moore, produced a sort of tribal-DIY-reclaimed aesthetic with reworked surplus clothes, found objects and bones and beads. (House of Beauty and Culture were the original vintage upcyclers, visionaries before their time.) Another member of the collective was Dave Baby, who specialised in phallic and vulvic totem poles, with a kind of Tiki look, and his work was hanging all over Crunch. To someone like me who had grown up in functional, but mostly undesigned domestic spaces, it was complete chaos, like being on another planet. I couldn't believe people lived that freely.

On weekends, Mark would throw a big Jamaican barbecue and invite the whole neighbourhood. The crowd included Rastafarians, punks and any number of Ladbroke Grove characters. Kate was always there with her boyfriend Mario Sorrenti, an Italian kid raised in New York who had come to London to model and started taking pictures. And Glen Luchford, a sharply dressed young blond from Brighton who was shooting for *The Face*, lived there for a spell as well.

Even when she was still a teenager, Kate was confident. Laughing, cracking jokes, smoking, at ease with everyone, full of charisma, yet down to earth. It never mattered to Kate whether the audience was five randoms at an afterparty or a thousand onlookers at a Versace show, she would have every last person in thrall. She danced and sang a lot, with a quite lovely voice. I was under her spell like everybody else, but hers wasn't an intimidating kind of allure. She was comforting and matey, with a thick, working-class accent and an engaging way of bringing me out of myself. There were always a lot of outfit changes with Kate, she had an innate way with clothes. Back then it was hipster jeans and vests and knits by Bella Freud. Then it became John Galliano slip dresses. And vintage – always vintage. She was as good at picking out second-hand stuff at Portobello Market as the stylists were.

The parties were fun, and we all talked endlessly about work. I was finding better ways to cover for my shyness, and in doing so, found my social circle expanding quickly. On any given night I had one of two red booths at 192, the Italian bistro in Notting Hill that defined the decade. There were times that I felt myself a part of the only world that mattered to me – a relief, given all the displacement I had lived through. But then there were times when I'd wake up in the morning and feel like the biggest fraud. With the wisdom of age and distance and experience, the lows make sense to me as a counterpoint to the almost unbearably high highs. But I'd have sporadic episodes of depression, which I pulled through by sheer will, because I didn't have time to indulge in maudlin, immobilising emotion. I was a man in perpetual motion. Staying home in bed wasn't an option. I could just knock back another drink and try to forget it, as both of my cultures, English and Ghanaian, dictated.

And I was always happier when I rolled up my sleeves. Commissioning the covers and pages, giving myself, and others in my young London world, free rein to explore what we thought was beautiful and modern and important to express, was exhilarating. It was 1991 and something was happening in fashion. This was the turn of a new aesthetic that would end up being called grunge.

For my part, I wanted to pare down the *i-D* of the 1990s. Make it more elemental and intimate, more personal and less abstract, more realistic and immediate. And as the person tasked to shape all the imagery, I was suddenly in a position to do it. I came into my own as a stylist as this avant-garde was peaking.

Let's not mince words: I was horrified by the commercial fashion imagery of the 1980s and all its tacky, contoured makeup and jumping ladies with plastic smiles. The supermodels like Christy Turlington and Linda Evangelista and Naomi Campbell, our homegrown London star, were amazing; it was nothing against the girls. It was just that the images and clothes were all so *Dynasty* and over the top and often phony. A triumph of fakery when what I yearned for was truth. In our grubby little corner of London, we remained in search of authenticity. Our generation was craving a sea change, and with the machinery of *i-D* behind me, I was going to give it to them.

Most people think of grunge today as an American post-punk genre of music, but it had a parallel ethos in fashion and it felt like the movement's ground zero was clustered around my desk. The aesthetic borrowed from punk, but with introspective melancholy and emotional vulnerability. Richard Avedon's resolutely unglamorous monograph, 'In the American West', was probably the most important visual and philosophical reference. The godfather of post-war haute-couture glamour was also one of the most searing cultural observers, and his series of black-and-white portraits of ex-cons, auto mechanics and waitresses shot in Texas in 1979 was a beacon guiding us away from strobe lights, shoulder pads and frosted hair. Other inspirations were Nan Goldin's derelict scenes, and the highly poetic Little England reportage of Martin Parr. And I was obsessed with Garry Winogrand, the photojournalist from the 1950s who pioneered street photography in New York.

We would remix all these photographic styles with vintage clothes and new-guard designers like Martin Margiela, twisting and slouching onto the models of the moment like Kate. *i-D* was the perfect setting for it. In our little indie magazine, other than that wink on the cover, models didn't have to smile or jump or sell much of anything. The world wasn't optimistic in the early 1990s and we saw no reason to try to push that. We were coming out of a period of right-wing political austerity, a time when we were ravaged by disease and the airwaves were dominated by a saccharine and pathetic TV culture. We wanted to shoot in playgrounds and school fields, cold British beaches and stripped-down rock-and-roll clubs in the harsh light of day. Our world – the real world – deserved to be seen. It had its own beauty and its time had come.

There was just one glaring problem for me. Most of what got to be called grunge was incredibly white. If this aesthetic vanguard was about realism and authenticity, my world, my real world, was not white. I felt the draw of this artistic moment like all of my peers. I was inspired by it and helped to form it. But for me, authentic reality included and often centred on Black women. So whenever it made sense to me, I cast them. I never felt any pushback from Terry or Nick over my choices of Black cover models, but as I started to hit my stride at *i-D*, a few people around the office would say, 'Oh, another one?' when they'd see a beautiful Black woman on the cover. Yes, another one. And another. There was endless Black beauty in the world that deserved to be on our covers.

Domestically, my life had a touch of the nomad. (Maybe the best training for living out of a suitcase, as all working stylists end up doing, was being a refugee.) When Michael got word that his father was returning to London, the two of us got the bright idea to move in with Judy Blame. We had enough money to pay a little bit of rent, and Judy was living in a large Victorian terraced house on Mortimer Road in Kensal Green, conveniently situated near Crunch, with spare bedrooms. The place had been loaned to him by Neneh Cherry, who had another flat in Camden where she and her growing family were living.

Chez Judy was a total mood. There were echoes of Crunch in how he had done up the house, with loads of Dave Baby and Frick and Frack. Safety pins were one of his signatures, and they were everywhere, in tapestries and collages. He also had a massive throne in the living room, from which he ironically, but not entirely ironically, held court. Judy was gregarious and quippy and smart as hell, with a proper education for all his punk credentials, including a deep knowledge and appreciation of art history.

People were always coming around to the house to plonk down in the living room and brainstorm with him. Björk wanted Judy to style her. The music producer Nellee Hooper, who was getting famous with Soul II Soul, would be pitching acts. Mark Lebon would be there, or Kate or Neneh or the photographer Jean-Baptiste Mondino. There was a fair amount of drug taking, and from morning till night, Judy always had a drink in hand. I wonder sometimes if he did it to calm his overactive mind. As social as he was, like us, Judy's creative synapses never stopped firing, and he basically never stopped working. He was always sketching or cutting or safety-pinning something onto something else, or leafing through a picture book or sizing up a piece of fabric or an intriguing set of buttons.

In Judy's parlance, his new flatmates, Michael and I, were 'the Africans'. As in, 'Oh don't bother clearing the table, the Africans will get it.' We responded by never clearing the table and telling him to sod off. One night out with me and Luther and Michael, the door person warned Judy not to go in with us or he might get mugged. 'These are my Africans!' he'd say. We allowed it. We were having fun living at party central, even if sometimes it was a bit much for me. I remember coming home from a club late one night, high on LSD, which made all the safety pins and Frick and Frack pretty alarming. I was still seeing things the next morning. Unaware I was likely still quite high, I called my mother. That's what you do when you're scared, and I had questions.

'Mum,' I said, 'when I look at the lightbulbs, I see the Bee Gees turning into skeletons.'

Pause.

'Have you tried any vodka?' she finally asked. 'Because that would be the reason why.'

'Yeah, I did.'

'Asiamah. Be careful.'

'OK.'

What she didn't know wouldn't hurt her.

Now that I was able to commission myself to style as much as I wanted, I called on Craig McDean, who was just starting to shoot on his own after a few years of assisting Nick Knight. Craig's technical rigour and painterliness appealed to me. Even as our aesthetic moment was coming into focus as gritty and socially realist, I was always drawn to polished, graphic, clean images. Craig's ability to render eccentricity with the clarity and poise of Vermeer felt elegant and cool and perfectly dosed. The more out there the clothes or the concept got, the frostier Craig got in the image. He understood composition and content and emotion and mood and, better than almost anyone else, especially for one so early in his career, lighting. He was a minimalist in the truest, finest sense of the word — whatever subtle thing he focused on, he gave it his full attention and elevated it in the process.

Craig was from the north of England, a college dropout who was obsessed with David Bowie and the Smiths and avant-garde fashion. He got his job with Nick by cold calling him and then eventually moving into his house. His talent and intensity and work ethic were apparent immediately. He loved motorcycles and racing cars and martial arts and the Bauhaus and, like Bowie, his choppy hair went from orange to magenta and back again. He was mumbly, reserved to the point of being impermeable, but I recognised the same fundamental shyness in him as I had in myself. As soon as he went out on his own, Craig started shooting album covers, which was a way a lot of the i-D set made their money.

Meanwhile, Michael had been working with a makeup artist called Pat McGrath. I kept hearing about her. And then Pat came into the office not long after I got the job, on the arm of a stylist called Zoe Bedeaux. Zoe looked like a cross between Sade and an African tribal warrior, and was starting to graduate from assisting Judy to doing her own work with Juergen, so anyone she endorsed had sway. But Pat could have come in with the postman and I would have taken notice.

I have only felt this a handful of times in my life, but I knew immediately when Pat turned up that it was destiny calling. Where I still practically spoke in a whisper, she was a bullhorn. She was small in stature but everything else about her was big: her eyes, her mouth, her laughter, which was infectious, warm and constant. She cracked herself up all the time. I remember I was in the middle of a conversation with someone in the office about upcoming articles, and a few seconds after we were introduced, Pat blurted out, 'You should do an article on me.' Cheeky and funny, sure, but I would soon learn there were multitudes to back up the attitude.

When she was growing up in Northampton, Pat was the only Black girl at her white school. She became obsessed with the Blitz nightclub, where Judy and Boy George and Leigh Bowery strutted around in Kabuki faces in the 1980s. As a makeup artist, even starting out, she had an innate graphic sensibility and one of the most focused eyes, practically like a second camera lens. Pat harnesses colour like an alchemist bringing down fire from the heavens, but she is also the most gifted person working today when it comes to subtlety and skin texture. I can't think of another makeup artist with her talent and vision and breadth, her ability to dispense drama perfectly, her ability to transform models with flashes of boundless inspiration.

Pat was one of the few Black creatives in our world back then who had mounting buzz around her. Unlike me, she held people's attention without hesitation or apology. She lived for beauty and understood the hard work and leaps of faith that it took to breathe it into life. In that respect, and perhaps in that respect alone, she was like my mother. Pat has turned out to be probably the single most impactful makeup artist in the history of fashion. To be there on the ground floor with her, finding our way through the industry together, was a gift.

Slowly a core gang started to form. Craig and Pat and I started working together on covers and portraits, like one we did of a champion diver I knew from Crystal Palace called Jason Statham. (He'd go on to become one of the biggest action-movie stars in the world.) Sometimes Michael would do the hair, but more and more we started working with a kid called Eugene Souleiman. Eugene was a ray of sunshine and a bit of a lad, in a rock band on the side. On sets you have a lot of downtime. While one team member is working on a model, the others wait. If Pat or Craig had their hands full and we were just waiting around, Eugene would try to scandalise me by egregiously farting and describing women's genitals in detail. Now approaching his august years, he's left the farting behind, but as much as I love his endless brilliance as a hair stylist, I love Eugene's warmth and total lack of pretension even more.

We'd work a lot at Metro Studios around the corner from i-D's offices. Photo studios are mostly just giant sheds with high ceilings that can be transformed into something else. Metro had two floors, and we often had the run of the place. i-D never had any budget for shoots, so we'd pool our money and get takeaway fish and chips or curry, or Pat, who was earning better than any of us, thanks to her steady work in the music business, would treat us to KFC or triangle sandwiches and beer from the newsagent. Except for Pat, who was always better behaved than us, we drank a lot of beer.

Eugene and Pat always showed up with massive cases, his full of hairpieces and sticks and bones and charms and bits of lace and tons and tons of lacquers and pastes, hers with brushes and greases and pots of pigment, and piles of bindis and charms, and anything else that could create an otherworldly impression on a face. Pat loved to smudge pigments onto her hands to show us the result before she went further. She was always shoving her hands in our faces to pitch us something like a fire-engine-red slash or dewy softness that glowed on her cocoa skin. I'd bring in the clothes in black bin bags: pieces from designers, vintage finds from Portobello Market and my ever-growing archive of 'stylist's own' pieces – a personal archive of irreplaceable items that got no credit on the pages but often made the difference in the picture. As soon as I arrived, I would arrange all the clothes onto racks, and begin steaming, so that everything I had was ready to go at a moment's notice, while Craig and his assistant would begin building and testing the lighting. Music would always be on – with Craig it was Bowie, the Clash, Primal Scream, the Cure, though we'd also let the model pick if it helped her get into the mood.

Once the model arrived, I'd often be the first one to welcome her, and start talking her through the mood boards, looking at the clothes and discussing the character. After trying on looks, fitting and Polaroiding so that I could present them to Craig, I'd hand her over to Eugene, who would then take hours to sculpt the hair, before Pat would have her turn. In my experience, there is no more precise, graphic, technical perfectionist than Eugene. In the early 1990s in our world, there was often very minimal, lanky, greasy hair. But Eugene brought so much vision and intellectual complexity to his work, he pushed past it. The results were always worth it, even if we'd go half mad waiting for them. If I wasn't gossiping with Pat while we waited for Eugene to finish up, I slept off a lot of hangovers on the couches while he teased and twiddled.

Craig, Pat, Eugene and I shared a love of kooky surrealist gestures, graphic colour and clean images. Even if I loaded on the social commentary in the shoot inspiration, Pat and Eugene's assertive input was my first lesson that sometimes clothes were just another ingredient in the hot soup of an image. Sometimes Eugene and Pat were so over the top that I needed to pull back on the styling for the greater good, to keep some simplicity. The mood of the moment was usually casual, anyway; we were reflecting the world around us. And I wasn't there to draw attention to myself – the important thing was the overall picture.

Like a family, we had our roles: Pat the joyful mum, Eugene the joker, Craig the withdrawn intense one, and sensitive little me overseeing everything. Dedication to the work and making our statement was what guided us, but in the course of getting there, we could yell and scream at each other if one of us felt the image wasn't working. There can be a lot of tension on a photoshoot, especially in the first couple of hours or days before you find your groove. As rigorous as my research and casting and character development was, those first few looks are always like pancakes. You need to be ready to throw them out. I would call this process 'the search'. Once you reach the first image where everybody is happy, then the search is over and you're rolling. But since time is limited, until you lock into a mood that works in real time on a particular model, it can feel like a long and arduous process. If one of us didn't like what the other was doing, it wasn't uncommon to rip test Polaroids into pieces. By the time the character was resolved, though, we were all in love again.

For all my sensitivity, the yelling didn't faze me. I might have been shy, but other than my mother, a bit of bluster was normal in my world. And as highly emotional as fashion can get, it wasn't scary the way my father was. Craig could be a devilish little underminer when he wanted to set me off, though. 'No matter what everyone else says about you,' he'd say to me, 'I think you're all right.' Oh really? Thanks. Pat was much softer. We'd be on set, talking all day and then I'd go back to Judy's and get on the phone with her and talk for five more hours afterwards. She was more strait-laced than Craig and Eugene and me, but she became a protector when I needed someone to talk to, a crucial kind of support now that I no longer had my mother around. Pat understood human relationships and had a great deal of emotional intelligence. As I was still so young and immature, I benefited a lot from her sound advice and sharp read on people.

Every now and then I had sickle-cell crises flare up – and my related thalassaemia diagnosis meant an increased tendency to severe pain episodes. The pain would start in the joints, like my fingers or knee, but then it would shoot down my legs like sciatica, and it could hobble me for up to ten days at a time. Walking became a chore. I didn't have too many debilitating crises by then, but when they hit, I tried to hide them. You can't take time for yourself when the clock is ticking and the team is waiting; you have to soldier on. I could be honest with Pat, though. One time it was so bad, she called an ambulance to get me to the hospital so I could get morphine, the only thing that really ever takes the pain away.

I have always been someone who would do anything in the name of his craft, which meant sometimes I do too much. But at the time I could sense that I was living through a crucial moment in fashion's evolution – we all knew – and I was damned if I was going to miss a second of it. The authenticity we strived to capture in images, both in the narrative idea for a shoot and by homing in on a model's most unique, sometimes even strange features, was all part of an ethos that celebrated raw individuality. The inspiration was gushing out like a firehose and we were there to try to catch it as it landed.

Craig, Pat, Eugene and I were spoiled in a way, and certainly by the models we worked with, who did as much to make the pictures great as we did. *i-D* was a scrappy little indie, cool with youth credibility, and so if we played our cards right, the marquee names who were bored stiff with Revlon contracts would come and shoot with us. We offered a chance to be a part of something more interesting than they'd find in the big, grown-up commercial world. Don't forget most models are *young* – and they always have been. The women of the moment like Kate and Naomi were our age, part of our generation. Doing a shoot with us in a poky studio with terrible food was way more fun than having to be on your best behaviour for *Vogue*. I was hungry to get the best models possible, and an *i-D* cover was becoming a must-have not just for up-and-coming girls, but the supers like Linda Evangelista and Christy Turlington.

The right model brings so much to a shoot. Linda brings poise, Naomi packs energy, Christy radiates serenity. Their spontaneity, expression and intelligent way of moving their faces and bodies are essential ingredients for the alchemy of a fashion image. I tended to work from a place of borderline obsessive love. If I loved you, I wanted to work with you over and over.

This was definitely true for Kate, who was such a stalwart collaborator. She'd arrive on set in the morning already so stylish in a bias-cut dress or a pair of tight jeans and a vest, and we'd go straight to the racks together. 'Should we make it shorter, should we do it with flats?' You'd bring her into the conversation as soon as possible, because from the very beginning she knew what worked best on her. Once the shoot got going, she'd always put a twist on her character. If the idea was to be a jazz singer, she'd want to listen to rock. Anything to avoid imitation and cliché. She could express everything in the crook of her little finger. If you're going to be a minimalist, whether as a designer or a photographer or a model, like Kate, a lot rests on small gestures. Kate always nailed them.

And then there was Lorraine Pascale, with her wide-open, sunny, gap-toothed smile. Of Jamaican and St Lucian descent, she was adopted into a white family in Oxfordshire, where she was discovered while bagging groceries at a supermarket, though when I first saw her in person, she had already moved to Ladbroke Grove. Her attenuated silhouette was perfect for the runway, her personality refined and elegant but with a welcoming quality. Along with Naomi, Lorraine was one of the first big Black models of our era. (She was on her way to a first-name-only career when she gave it up to become a celebrity chef, and now a shrink, which was probably always her truest calling.) Along with her beaming charisma, Lorraine had a beautiful fragility that you just wanted to protect. Craig and Pat were obsessed with her luminous skin and I loved all the confessional conversations in our downtime. The subject was always spirituality, or self-help, or psychology, never fashion.

Coming up in London, Lorraine suffered a lot from the unbearable whiteness of grunge. About five years after we first started working together, she had had it with fashion. She told me about all the shoots she was booked on where she'd show up thinking it was for a chic magazine and a chic assignment, and the accessories table would just be cowrie shells and bones. I couldn't understand how anyone could limit Lorraine's range of expression – she was capable of so much – but then the big commercial magazines had, since the 1970s, established a habit of depicting African and Black women as undiscovered and 'exotic'. How many white models got sent onto big-budget shoots in African countries where beautiful local people would be cast as undifferentiated backdrops for their colonial adventures? How many Black women with as much to offer as Lorraine had to keep smiling and bugging out their eyes?

i-D specialised in London girls like Kate and Lorraine. But it was Naomi who, more than any other model, just made my head explode. She was the only one of that generation I recognised from before I got into fashion. (My sister Mina really did resemble her when we were kids.) We were desperate to shoot her for i-D. I wanted to transform her from the big 1980s glamazon into something weirder and more unexpected.

In our now thirty years of working together, in my hands Naomi has become Elvis and David Bowie, Marie Antoinette and a frustrated flapper, and so many other personae not usually accorded to Black women. And there is no end to what Naomi is capable of. If they say we're only tapping into 10 per cent of what the human brain can do, fashion has still only scratched Naomi's surface. Her ability to bring fire to any character gave me the freedom to let my imagination run wild. And she has been a muse to many people in fashion: Azzedine Alaïa, Domenico Dolce and Stefano Gabbana, Gianni Versace and later Donatella too. And very much, me.

The first time I met Naomi properly was in 1993, when I had finally booked her to do a cover shoot with Jeny Howorth, a model-turned-photographer who was a good friend of hers. We went to pick her up after the Chanel show in Paris, the same season she fell off those notorious Vivienne

Westwood platform shoes on the catwalk. She came out from
backstage in an Anna Sui slip dress and a wet, curly, Whitney
Houston-inspired bob, having just washed her hair. She was
so charming, and excitable, like a little girl. She spoke to me
like I was already an old friend. 'You have to come to Dublin
with me after the shoot!' she pressed, maybe five minutes
after we first shook hands. (She was dating Adam Clayton
from U2 then.) What little money I had in my pocket was
borrowed. Maybe next time?

The clothes on that shoot were simple – we wanted
freshness, spontaneity, understatement. Jeny had a vintage
bias-cut dress that she loaned us and I took a pair of scissors
and chopped off the bottom. Jeny was furious, but the dress
made the cover. What was so interesting about Naomi on
that shoot, and all the ones since, was her self-assurance. She
never wanted to look at Polaroids to see what we were seeing;
she just wanted to work. She was there to perform, and to
exchange with us, she didn't need to check in and validate the
progression of the shoot. If she agreed to work with us, she
was going to give us her trust.

I've probably shot more with Naomi than any other
model, and she quickly became a friend. Along with Pat, she
was the most successful high-profile Black woman in fashion at
the time, and for me, she was the ultimate port in the storm.
Then as now, she was assertive, and knew her own value. She
has an elephant's memory and protects her friends. Like Pat,
she was an important example to me then that Black people

can be the centre of the universe and that we can do things on our own terms. But no one is going to create that space for us. We have always had to do that for ourselves. Naomi is always on the phone all day making things happen, pushing, cajoling, charming. For herself and for the good of others.

Meanwhile, the stylists I was getting around the table at meetings to pitch me at *i-D* were starting to make real, serious money working outside of magazine editorials, getting on planes, seeing the world. Yet here I was under a bare lightbulb at the office, writing shopping pages and asking Judy for spare change when I couldn't pay for my own spaghetti alle vongole at 192. Simon put me up for some jobs, and the record companies would hire me to work with visiting R&B bands or new-look gospel ones like Sounds of Blackness. But it was becoming clear to me that fashion's main players were having a far easier time imagining white women stylists as a fit for the top consulting jobs. I wasn't trusted in the same ways they were, or included in the same conversations, or seen as the big creative contributor in the ways that my editorial work should have made obvious. How ironic. *i-D* was evolving into an era-defining magazine with my leadership of the fashion department. Terry was giving me a long leash, and the work we were turning out as a team looked ever more sophisticated and fashion-forward, and yet when it came time to hire a consulting stylist for the big commercial jobs? Crickets.

I contributed to the problem in my own way. I was not great at selling myself. As a Black person in a still very white world, I knew I had to keep it humble. It was an ego-boost for me and a relief to my colleagues that I could take so much on my shoulders, but it had an adverse effect on my mind and soul. When you can do all things for all people, and well enough to be consistently rewarded for it, especially from a very young age, you have a harder time landing on what actually makes you, yourself tick. It becomes about what you can do for others, and when you can do whatever that is to a high standard, and you're young, a perverse system of incentives gets installed in you. You bend to the situation, you don't impose yourself on it. You see yourself as of service to the talent rather than the talent yourself. It can make you feel empty inside, when you know that somewhere within you there's more to say. I know one of the reasons I was on the run so much, working myself ragged, going from office to club to set to office to club to party, was because I felt I could work my way out of any problem, no matter how existential or intractable. And then to soften the blow, or more easily find the laughter or outgoing response that was called for, I would drink.

It didn't help me stay true to my own compass. I was so eager to learn and experiment, to collaborate with strong creative partners, that even as I felt myself developing a style of my own, it might have read to others as too broad, too hard to pinpoint. From my perspective today, that breadth is how I'm able to edit one magazine and oversee the output of an entire continent of *Vogue* editions. But back then it was another reason, along with the deeply entrenched racism of the fashion industry, that I wasn't breaking out when they were. I was in too many places at once, and not fully there wherever I was.

In addition to the start of my friendship with Naomi, 1993 was the year that Kate's iconic Obsession ads shot by Mario Sorrenti ran, and suddenly she was the biggest model in the world. As such, she was also a beacon of controversy. She was anorexic, they said. She was a junkie, they said. She was none of those things, of course, but she was making headlines in the tabloids with the new visibility that Calvin Klein gave her. The photographers who shot her back in London got even more respect, and higher-profile work, than before.

Calvin Klein was evolving as a designer into the American representative of the same aesthetic we all loved: androgynous, cool minimalism. There was Helmut Lang in Paris, Jil Sander in Hamburg, Prada in Milan, and Calvin in America, and he had more money than all of them put together. In 1994, he made another push into the stratosphere with the launch of CK One, a unisex fragrance targeted at young people. The American photographer Steven Meisel, whom Pat idolised, was hired to shoot the campaign, with Kate out front as usual.

New York was calling Craig and Pat, too. Even if London was an acknowledged source of creativity, America was where the money was. It represented more limitless opportunity compared to the UK, where a working-class accent or not having gone to the right school, let alone, like in Pat's case, your skin colour, could be enough to stymie your progress. *Women's Wear Daily* decided to spin off their insert, called *W*, into a standalone magazine, and Craig went off to work for them, moving to New York. It was large format, to give an outlet to edgier photographers. When he took a white stylist from *Harpers & Queen* on those jobs and not me, I didn't speak to him for months.

Meanwhile, I kept my nose to the grindstone, and reached out to other photographers, of whom there were many: the incredible, otherworldly Paolo Roversi, the portrait genius Richard Burbridge, and Juergen, with whom I did one of my favourite shoots with Kristen McMenamy, an absolute daredevil, in 1996. She had just lost an option for a Versace campaign shot by Avedon, and had broken her collarbone, when she came to London to do a cover for us. We had captured our shot, and as Juergen and Kristen were talking shit about Versace – sour grapes in the moment, it's normal – in a moment of protest, I grabbed Kristen's own lipstick and scrawled 'Versace' across her chest as Juergen snapped away. Juergen won't ever retouch photos, and her visible bruises and full-frontal nudity were raw and unabashed. Those pictures were scandalous.

Sometimes I'd take a side job, say if Patti Wilson wanted my help on a shoot for *Vibe* magazine in New York. Patti was literally the first Black stylist in America. She created legendary images with the photographer Bill King in the 80s and 90s, and she'd let me sleep on her floor when I was in town. This made working on location for *i-D* possible for me.

The day of one memorable *i-D* shoot, I headed to the Meatpacking District with Steven Klein to photograph Kate and Naomi. This was back when that neighbourhood was still a hangout for New York's alternative drag scene. I'll never forget the sight of a group of queens clocking Kate and Naomi and then heading straight over to impart a lesson on how to walk and swing their purses. A match made in heaven. It was hard to tell who was schooling who.

I'm still so proud of the work I put out in that period, even if I can spot the growing pains. I was an integral part of a trove of iconic images that helped to change the tone and reach of the fashion industry at the time. Though I was growing resentful as everyone else was pulling ahead of me, I was too busy to let bitterness completely take me. We had a magazine to put out.

And then, finally, I got my chance. It didn't come through Craig, though he was booked to shoot it. It came through Ronnie Cooke Newhouse, who had gone from being a founder of the Downtown New York bible *Details* magazine to an art director at Calvin Klein. Calvin and Ronnie loved what we were doing at *i-D*, my agent told me. Could I come in for a meeting?

Yes, I could.

AMERICA

New York, 1996. Craig McDean, Ronnie Cooke Newhouse and me on set at Calvin Klein.

CHAPTER FIVE

Seven years after teenage me, armed with wild-eyed enthusiasm and those bicycle shorts, first touched down in New York with Simon to consult for Levi's, I found myself once again in Manhattan, strutting through Midtown, straight into the doors of Calvin Klein HQ. Well, I say 'strutting' – in truth, I was as nervous as hell. This was the moment I'd been waiting for, the sort of job that could take my career to the next level. But I also felt like I was coming full circle. My teenage self had been flattened by the sight of that ginormous Calvin Klein poster of Kate on the side of a building as I had crossed the 59th Street Bridge, and now here I was, in the then-undisputed centre of fashion power, on the way to make it happen. If it all went well, my work would be on that wall. My heart was in my throat.

Two years before I walked into my big meeting, Calvin Klein had launched CK for younger consumers. The fashion trade calls this kind of side brand a 'bridge line' because it's supposed to be a gateway to buying into the company's higher-end offer. Often this means a watered-down message, but Calvin had put massive creative and financial resources into CK's design and communications, funded by the influx of cash from having sold his highly profitable jeans and underwear businesses. At the time I walked through the doors, business-wise and creatively, Calvin was at his peak. He was one of the most successful American designers in the history of fashion, dominating the conversation of the moment through his clothes, and also especially his advertising, always right on point and laced with plenty of controversy.

The job I was called in for was to style a series of CK advertising campaigns, for which Kate was, again, the face. I'd be shooting with Craig, with Pat doing makeup and Eugene the hair: a creative safe space, even if I was still quietly furious at Craig. I was walking in with Ronnie's support – she was Calvin Klein's advertising and creative director. Her dry humour and sharp focus put me at ease from the first time I spoke with her. She knew and loved London, was friends with many of the original *i-D* crew, the furthest thing from square or corporate, and she was vocally a fan of my work. But whatever I did would need the blessing of Calvin himself.

I remember what I wore on that first day we met. I did my signature Fashion Director in jeans, a V-neck sweater with a white T-shirt underneath and a camel-hair coat from English Squire. Low-key but with a bit of polish. (When you're outside talent booked to consult, you're not expected to dress like everyone else, but you want to be more or less on the same planet.) Here I was, finally making a proper rate of thousands a day, like so many of my peers had been doing for years. I had been dying for this break and I knew I could deliver.

There is, however, another factor on days like these. I was well turned out, I had the experience and my preparation, as always, was nothing short of obsessive. Yet I also carried with me a different anxiety, a brand of anxiety that Craig or Eugene or Melanie Ward could never feel: a cloud that always hovers over a Black person in a new setting, especially one that is wealthy and white. An apprehension that is always just… there. Even if I was clearly in the minority at *i-D*, we were a scrappy little family with no money, and I was a central cog, known and trusted by everyone. Still, if I hadn't experienced overtly ill treatment at *i-D*, I had by this time lived for over a decade in the UK, where I'd had plenty of experience seeing people on the street clutching their bags when I walked by, or teachers dialling down their expectations of me in class, or men pigeonholing me in gay clubs, or colleagues assuming I was of lower professional status at designer showrooms and fashion shows where they didn't know me on sight, or police giving me the once-over. Yes, there had been many moments of joyful professional validation, and I knew that I benefited from breaks that no one, Black or white, had ever had. But on any given day, my life had been contoured by suspicion, hostility and double standards in ways both egregious and subtle. And now I was in New York, where police violence against Black men was even more extreme than what I had come to know in London. Rudolph Giuliani had been elected mayor in 1994 on a tough-on-crime platform that any Ladbroke Grove resident would have clocked in a second. The most outrageous incidences of racist police violence in New York – against Abner Louima, Amadou Diallo and Patrick Dorismond – were yet to come, but with the city and its financial industries on an extended sugar high, Giuliani had given aggressive, entitled white people permission to discriminate. New York was having a moment, but it was not a great vibe for Black people.

I waltzed into all this to get my big break at an iconic temple of American whiteness. CK was making waves with advertising that was ethnically diverse and gender fluid. But before that initiative, Calvin's iconography was as white as his staff, which mostly consisted of tall, bony, beautiful WASP girls with thick eyebrows and low ponytails. I could count the Black people inside the building on one hand, and they were almost all security guards. Otherwise there was one Asian producer. Quite a rainbow coalition.

In fashion, as elsewhere, establishment companies, almost all of them owned and run by white people, don't have to have an over-the-top, overtly racist culture for a Black worker to feel panic and fear upon arriving. It's an instinct we develop over a lifetime of being unfairly judged, and then gaslighted if we actually take the enormous risk of simply talking about our experiences. We know all the stereotypes about us intimately, and jump through hoops – social, psychological, emotional – to counteract them on the job. We know them because one of the most crucial survival skills for any Black person in a white space is to intimately understand how institutional white psychology works. In addition to knowing our own minds and hearts, we have to absorb the dominant culture, how it thinks and reacts.

To go into any white space without that comprehension is like walking into a sword fight without a rapier and a shield. You just don't do it. You have to master the mindset.

Look, don't get me wrong. Starting a new job is stressful for anyone, yet in contrast, white colleagues can at least show up more or less unburdened by preconceived notions of being lazy, crass, undereducated, unrefined, dishonest, shady, a diversity hire, short-fused or dying to accuse everyone else of being racist. Black people know, both by way of advice from our elders and our own experiences, that even from well-meaning white people we rarely, if ever, get the benefit of the doubt if a conflict arises. We know that we're often the first to be blamed, and more quickly and harshly punished than our white peers. If there was ever a question of an item of clothing or jewellery going missing at any job where I wasn't intimately known to the client, I'd be the first one they suspected, even if they liked me, because there's an unconscious tripwire in most white people that says, when it comes right down to it, Black people do not belong. And God forbid I get visibly angry about it. Or express any of my natural fear and insecurity. This emotional and psychological reality is exhausting on its own. Now combine it with knowing that you'll always need to work twice as hard to keep rising. Being Black in the workplace is not a recipe for inner peace.

There was another dip in this emotional rollercoaster for me. In America, I would get a bit more of a pass than my Black American peers, because my Englishness seemed 'classy'. To Americans, it associated me with stately homes, tea parties and the British Royal Family – clichés that operated outside the corrosive, centuries-old dynamic of America's own homegrown racist system. (The 'exotic foreign' thing works in reverse too. Black American artists like Ralph Ellison, Josephine Baker, Miles Davis and James Baldwin were spared some of the racism in France that people of colour from that country, or its colonies, experienced daily.) If only the people complimenting my accent or telling me I was somehow different knew what Black people in the UK went through, and how not-different it all was. If only they saw that the Jamaicans who came to the UK dealt with the same kind of discrimination as the ones who came to the US. I also knew that even with this odd good fortune, my God-given talent and my ambition to make something out of it, if I screwed up on anything it could all disappear in an instant. As it pertained to my industry, I was both privileged to have so many opportunities to shine at such a young age, and also underprivileged because of my accent and the colour of my skin. A mind fuck.

So I arrived at Calvin Klein simultaneously thrilled, eager to please and trepidatious, like a soldier in a war zone, knowing that even if the space was outwardly welcoming, no matter what I did, it was going to be far more of a minefield for me than it would have been for someone white.

It is what it is, I said to myself. I'm one outside consultant; I have no power to change this corporate culture.

Suck it up, keep going. And so I did, and it went well. But I swore to myself then, and have done so many times since, that once I was in a position to give opportunities to others, I would give other Black creatives the space and permission to flourish and stretch themselves on their own terms. When people are able to apply the best of themselves to their work, free from outdated, harmful prejudice, we get a much better result. The world is in too dire a need of creativity, of original thought, to hold anyone back who may have the next great idea, who could be helping us move forward together.

My natural reaction to the stress of this big break, as it has been during any time of uncertainty in my life, was to work harder. Work was my upbringing and nature. And it was a psychological shelter. In busying myself with inspiration, on a quest to push forward new ideas of beauty in our time, I also found a constructive outlet for the nervous tension caused by my insecurity and impostor syndrome. I put in countless hours of research on my own for this job. I wanted to be beyond prepared. Because I had very green assistants, I'd need to train them up. (For the first time in my life, I had full-time help reporting to me to haul and catalogue and steam clothes.) And as part of a team of three other scruffy London creatives learning to work with a multimillion-dollar business, I was not going to be the one to put a foot wrong. Even if my adrenaline was pumping, I would be quiet, thoughtful, focused, polite and let them see how hard and how well I worked. Tiredness, when it came, was just a side effect. Nothing that a night out at Sound Factory couldn't cure.

On my first day in that pristine white office, I was brought in to meet Zack Carr, Calvin's right hand. He was warm and welcoming – what a relief. He took me down to a bright, cavernous room where the clothes had been hung on racks in expectation of my arrival. It was a behemoth commercial collection, infinite-seeming in the volume of pieces and breadth of styles, a world away from the tightly edited runway collections I was used to working with for magazine styling. My job here would be to create thirty looks out of what I saw, which Calvin and the company's CEO, Gabriella Forte, would whittle down to fifteen that we'd actually shoot. Before coming to Calvin, Gabriella had been the much-feared CEO of Armani. She was rumoured to make grown men cry on a daily basis. Thankfully, I never got any smoke; she was always great to me.

The commercial imprimatur of the campaign – ensuring this collection sold in droves in stores around the globe – took precedence over our own fashion impulses. Meaning Craig, Pat, Eugene and I weren't there to create an over-the-top fantasy, but to inspire people to come into Calvin's world of ever-expanding acreage at department stores, and a growing number of his own boutiques, and spend their hard-earned money to achieve the dream of what they saw in our pictures. Customers needed to be able to relate to and buy what they were seeing. No opera, no retro, no princesses, no 'stylist's own' fripperies for added poetic effect. It was about distilling cool and ensuring real-world appeal. Even though we were technically following someone else's highly commercial agenda rather than our own unfiltered instincts, we were actually the perfect fit for this job.

The minute I entered that massive room, I went straight to the racks and started whipping through them to check out the clothes. That's what I was doing when Calvin walked through the door. He was tall, angular, elegant and laser-focused. I already knew from his reputation that he had no time for silliness. After we shook hands, he started pointing out pieces he liked especially, or knew would work well in certain regions of the country. (Calvin was a merchandising genius and knew on a granular level what would sell where.) I was obsessed with military style at the time, and CK had just launched CK Khakis, which I loved as much as he did.

Calvin told me about his view of minimalist luxury, and why Kate was such a perfect symbol of it. The more enthusiastic and inspired he got, the more he moved his hands around while he talked. With CK, he wanted to signify freedom, openness, fun. The woman he saw as emblematic of his brand was a love child, but one who was globally well-travelled and elegant. Kate was, for him, his most important front person since Brooke Shields. I laughed to myself at this view he had of our Ladbroke Grove around-the-way girl, and didn't say that I already knew her. Anyway, he wasn't wrong. Kate had become exactly what he described. As Calvin spoke, I continued to reach for pieces of clothing, which I'd examine, tug at and feel as he talked.

I had about three days to create my thirty looks, which my assistants and I first assembled on headless mannequins. (The process is called rigging.) CK's fashion director, Sidney Backman, and Gabriella then came and made their picks, and presented them to Calvin. For this job I leaned into elegance and polish. Kate would wear vests and khakis, but paired with kitten-heeled mules. The naivety and waifishness of grunge was starting to lose steam, and we were looking for something more sophisticated and sleek. Calvin approved. He loved layering T-shirts, which he'd ruche up and down the body to show off the different layers at the waist or the sleeve – they called it 'a slice'. It was a sharp way to colour-block, and sell more merchandise, so we sliced away.

The next step was the fittings, which we did directly on Kate. I was so happy to see her. Imagine you're hired to work at an intimidating, corporate fortress for the first time in your life, and you see your old mate from the afters who is now practically running things. I'd tell her when we were trying on looks, 'OK, come on Kate, I'm loving this one, so please tell them you love it too.' Over the two years I consulted for CK, some of the best times were when Gabriella would lock me and Kate and the collection in that big room and shout, 'Go create looks!' We tended not to love the suiting. Every time I brought out something tailored, she'd roll her eyes. Kate was already working for Calvin's main line, where the fabric was higher quality, so these felt a bit basic. And we wanted this to be young and rebellious. This work was so personal to us, especially to Kate, who was both conscientious of her relationship with her client and intimately associated with the brand.

For every look we'd try on, Kate would spend what felt like hours studying the angles in the mirror. She hiked things up, turned herself around and around, really testing and wearing the outfit. If she didn't feel it, and didn't feel like it was true to the character we were creating, we passed on it and went to another.

I'd never had to have my choices pre-approved before, but once we were on set, we took chances and improvised in the images, especially Pat. She put Kate in bold makeup, despite how the Calvin Klein of this era was very much about a nude face. She did dark berry lips and bronze eyes. Once she completely covered Kate's eyes in graphic black shadow. They had second thoughts and tried to retouch it out and it didn't work. The pictures ended up running, giving another dimension to the brand's visual language, helping it stretch and move beyond its hyper-naturalistic starting point. Like us, CK was growing up too.

I was in New York a lot now, finally with some money to burn. Calvin booked rooms for us all at the Soho Grand Hotel, including Kate, even though she already had an apartment in town. The Soho Grand had recently opened, the first boutique hotel of the Ian Schrager type but located Downtown, where all the fun was. It was the first time I'd ever been put up in such a slick place, and I loved it. It had a DJ in the lobby and once we got upstairs after work, we'd hop from room to room, having drinks before we went out for the night. The hotel was perfectly adjacent to New York institutions like Odeon and Lucky Strike, French bistros whose studied casualness and steady clientele of boldfaced names reminded me a little of 192 back in London. We went to gay dive bars like the Boiler Room in the East Village, the drag parties at Don Hill's in the Meatpacking District, and nights like Beige, which was every Tuesday at Bowery Bar, a capacious indoor-outdoor restaurant that was rapidly recolonising a once-dilapidated stretch of the East Village.

The brightest and most creative part of the New York nightlife carnival never missed Beige. It was drag queens and rock stars, Downtown personalities, supermodels and fashion designers. The best tables had impossibly deep banquettes, where lesser mortals would pass by and gawk or pay their respects. My little posse on these nights usually included the designer Narciso Rodriguez, and Paul Rowland, who was Kate's booker at Women, the agency he founded. By this time stretch limos were a thing, and Kate had one at her disposal, as did Naomi and new supers Amber Valletta and Shalom Harlow. Kate and Naomi had become as thick as thieves by now and could set any room anywhere on fire just by walking in the door. Paparazzi trailed them. It was the first time I saw how truly relentless being famous could be.

Beige was an all-night affair, and if you knew where to look, drugs were easy to get. They provided an efficient way out of the shyness that continued to plague me. Out in these increasingly glamorous settings, people started to discover another side of me. 'I never knew you were funny, Edward!' was something I heard a lot around that time. Being in the company of famous models, champagne flowed steadily too, whether the house was paying, or they were, or I was. I had already established a round-the-clock rhythm at *i-D*, where I had just gone freelance so I could accommodate Calvin and jobs for other designers that were starting to come in. It's just the dinners and the parties were now getting fancier and more frequent.

If I needed to take a break, I could always go around to Pat's apartment in the West Village and order takeout and watch a movie. She and Michael Boadi had moved full time to New York by then too, as well as Craig. We teased Pat for being a goody-goody, but her place was a refuge. I was in New York maybe one week out of four, and I had also started seeing a freelance photographer who I'd met at the printer where he worked: Lexington Labs. Having someone who resembled a boyfriend was like being granted a long-held wish, though it meant I was even more tired when I went into work. Thankfully our set atmosphere was permissive enough, especially if I was on an *i-D* shoot, that I could catch up on sleep there if I had to. A quiet corner and forty winks. What more could you need?

While my freelance consulting gigs were getting better and better, I was still hungry to create with the best of the best. To fashion and photography lovers like me, *Vogue* Italia was the holy grail. And Craig – alongside his advertising jobs and look books for designers like Jil Sander – was now contributing there. This magazine may not have had the massive circulation of American *Vogue*, but Franca Sozzani, the editor-in-chief, believed ardently in photographers and stylists as artists and oracles, and had eccentric enough taste to allow magic to occur on her pages. She loved high concepts and gave Steven Meisel free rein to do his most creative and visionary work, with pages and pages devoted to his creations, so each issue was a discovery. Pat was already starting to split her time between Craig and Steven, which drove Craig crazy with jealousy. Of course, I loved that.

My desire to work for *Vogue* Italia was reaching the level of desperation, and finally Craig put me forward for a story I pitched him called 'Walking'. Being in New York had inspired me immensely. Its creativity and energy and diversity percolated in me. So much of its life is lived out on the street, which I have always loved to chronicle. I was struck by how professional New York women would charge around town in trainers, with a pair of heels in their bag, and wanted to do a fashion take. Franca approved the idea, made sure we were including the right mix of designers, and off we went to do coats and long skirts and flat sandals on Maggie Rizer and Heather Stohler and some other new faces, running chicly to and fro in the Meatpacking District and around Wall Street, with a huge fan blowing at them like a tornado.

Those moments shooting out on the street are always a bit precarious. Anything could happen. In a city that stops for no one, passers-by stopped and stared.

Even though Craig and I loved the results of the story, and Franca had already approved the concept, I didn't know her at all, and was panicked the night before we sent it in, convinced she'd hate it. Was the concept strong enough? Was the wind machine too nuts? Did it look amateurish? Was it chic enough?

Thankfully, we soon found out, it was chic enough. Franca loved it. Not too long after Craig and I handed that story in, I was at a party in Milan during Fashion Week, where I had styled the runway show for Alessandro Dell'Acqua, and I spotted Franca. With her Botticelli-blonde curls and Balenciaga coat, she was hard to mistake for anyone other than her sister, Carla, the gallerist and fashion buyer behind the influential 10 Corso Como boutique. I wanted to get a moment in person with her, so I walked by and said hello, and she shot me a look of death. I scurried off back to a corner and rejoined Alek Wek, the Sudanese model – really the first Dinka model in fashion – whom I had come in with. (I first met Alek in London when she was sixteen, and I had picked up a styling job on a Burger King commercial.) I asked Alek if she'd properly introduce me to Franca. She said of course, and walked me over. 'Franca,' she said, 'this is my friend Edward Enninful.' Franca's whole face lit up. 'Edward Enninful the stylist? My God, I love your work!'

I took that moment of encouragement and ran with it. I got in touch with Franca's office and started to pitch her directly, working to stretch my mind with references and historic time periods and settings I wouldn't usually consider at *i-D*. From that moment on, I never had to go through a photographer to get a story into *Vogue* Italia again. I'd send her emails proposing Fellini girls on the beach, or portraits of interesting real women I knew, or up-and-coming musicians – she said yes to everything. I was like a kid in a candy store. To have won the trust and approval of such an icon was a massive feather in my cap. While my impostor syndrome was never far away, Franca's confidence in me meant I could relax a little and just lean into my imagination, which was running wild now that it had an outlet in one of the greenest pastures I had yet to encounter. *Vogue* Italia emphasised hardcore fashion more than celebrity, but I wanted to feature women I felt had something to say – an impulse that has only grown in me as time has passed. Franca could see the inspiration in big ideas but also simple ones, like the time Craig and I shot his then-girlfriend, a model called Carmen Hawk, just hanging around their apartment. Craig could always find the poetry in small moments.

The page count for fashion stories at *Vogue* Italia often went into the double digits, which meant more clothes per shoot, and more narrative pathways for my mythical superwomen. We'd photograph Naomi in a studio as a 60s ingénue, but instead of the lavish prints we got from the printer, we photocopied them and ran those in the magazine. (Terry's love of putting an image through multiple processes had left its mark on us.) Or we'd pack up a crew and travel to Tulsa to shoot Amber Valletta like David Bowie in *The Man Who Fell to Earth*.

Another thing that Franca's faith in me enabled was to allow me to step into a place of authority. In addition to Craig, I shot with a lot of the photographers I already knew well from *i-D*, like Paolo Roversi and Steven Klein, so I had this magical, creative comfort zone, a base that allowed me to hone a more elevated approach as a stylist. And there was a new generation of models coming up too, who, for the first time in my professional experience, were younger than me. Next to the Belgian Hannelore Knuts, a dark-haired Patti Smith-looking prodigy everyone was obsessed with, and the Brazilian bombshell Gisele Bündchen and Isabeli Fontana, with her handsome square jaw, also just arrived from Brazil, I felt wise and old and experienced. It was a welcome change from being the young whippersnapper trying to figure it all out on the job.

Two years after we started at Calvin Klein, the CK brand went back to using Steven Meisel, whose stylist was Joe McKenna. This was the end of our CK run, an episode that my stylist peers and I called 'the hirings and the firings'. 'Twas ever thus in fashion. As a freelancer, you work with a client for a while, and then even if they love your work, they feel the winds change, and move on to someone else to bring in a new energy. Since you're not an employee, you're not often warned in advance; your agent just doesn't get the call for the next job. Half the time you find out who the new team is through the rumour mill at a party. Cheers!

If you want to overanalyse the past, you can torture yourself over why you didn't get a call back. You can second-guess every conversation with the client or worry that maybe you just didn't always find the spark, even if the pictures are proof that you almost always did. Thankfully, I didn't have time to brood. *Vogue* Italia and Calvin were high-profile launching pads. Other designers, like Dell'Acqua, and Missoni and Trussardi and the menswear brand Richard Edwards, filled the financial holes I felt after losing Calvin's lovely American day rates. And I had also started to contribute to the just-launched *Vogue* Japan, thanks to a boost from Ronnie, who made sure her husband Jonathan Newhouse, head of Condé Nast International, knew I could be trusted to deliver. Editorial didn't pay nearly as much, but the agenda was simpler, and more creatively free. As I got more comfortable with the world of commercial styling, where you work to enhance the output of one single designer, I began to savour the magazine jobs more and more, where I could put things together according to my own instincts, to chronicle the times, to shape the future as I saw it, rather than execute someone else's vision.

Back in London, where I was still in charge of *i-D*'s fashion output, grinding out the pages in the office one week a month, I finally had my own flat, on the third floor of St Marks Road at Notting Hill Gate. It was a three-bedroom with a mezzanine, bigger than anything I'd ever lived in alone

— though the perfect size for the afterparties that seemed to magically materialise in my sitting room. I didn't fill the place out too much. I've never been big on fancy furnishings. I wasn't home enough to appreciate art on the walls or elaborate colour schemes, and had enough going on in my head. I had a TV and bean bags, papers and Polaroids. Other than that, I simply craved a blank slate.

I was so proud of this place, though. It was tangible proof that all my years of work and sacrifice had paid off. It proved my father wrong. He always told me I'd end up coming back home like a prodigal son. Instead, I was starting to send money home to help out and living well on my own. I didn't have to struggle every month. I could even provide for a partner.

I met Uwe at Heaven (of course) in 1998. He was German, an electropop musician, very tall and handsome, with a proud regal nose and a shaved head. We spotted each other at the bar and got talking. He had just moved to London from Berlin and worked with computers. He was the first person to explain to me what this email thing was. He was super-left-wing, and radically racially conscious for a white man. Even at the end of the 90s, Britain was still awash in prejudice against the Germans, a small-minded hangover over from the Second World War, so Uwe felt the backhand of bigotry himself, even if it wasn't quite the same as what I went through.

He moved in to the St Marks Road flat and I was so happy to be with him that I convinced myself I was willing to shed my more carefree habits, or at least to try. I wouldn't go out and party so much; I wouldn't drink until all hours of the night or have quite so many people trail me home after the clubs. He was a vegan, so I became one too. (I had hardly given food much thought in the workaholic 90s, so the transition wasn't that bad.) Something in me hoped he'd rescue me from the fast pace and the rootlessness that career success was causing. But I knew, for all my pride in my new home, I was unmoored from it. If I wasn't really able to calm myself down, even with that outward measure of security, how was he going to? And how could I say no to the temptation of getting on another plane to shoot Naomi somewhere?

During the three years we were together, I started out with the best of intentions, but eventually I chafed at the restrictions I had put on myself in his name. After we established our rather chaste domestic rhythm – dinner at home, quiet nights in – when I started to feel hemmed in or bored, I would drink in secret. Not that I had a problem, I told myself. He was just a scold, and I didn't want to deal with his disapproval. Also, my friends were not nice to him. Even if they knew this was real love for me – and for the first time ever, something I had wanted so much – they didn't welcome him. Did they sense something I didn't? Mixing Uwe in on nights out with my gang was awkward and eventually it only created more distance between us. He didn't love fashion, so he didn't really get what motivated them either, and yet he was understandably sensitive to their rejection. Sometimes he took it out on me, telling me they didn't really love me, that only he did. For the first time in my young life, I started to put on weight.

We were both immature. I felt guilty for hiding from him, which was compounded by the fact that I was hiding from my family too. And I flat out hated myself for that. I made excuses all the time not to go round and see my mother, even if I should only have been proud of what I'd made of myself since my father threw me out. But I felt rundown and self-conscious and phony around her when I did see her. She'd often complain that I didn't call enough, that I left her, that I wasn't eating enough, and so my mind escaped to the next flight to somewhere far away, the next killer concept, the next exciting model. Like with Uwe, when I would see my mother, I was there but not there. Also, I didn't want her to see me hungover. So rather than arrange a time when maybe I could drop by to the house for a visit, assured my father wouldn't be there, I complained to everyone how busy I was and kept my distance more than I should have. I was stuck in a cycle of avoiding the people I cared most about. Rinse and repeat.

I'll tell you what: nothing aids self-delusion like a jam-packed schedule. In 2001 came my first proper designer consulting job at Jil Sander. The Prada Group had bought it and installed me and Miuccia Prada's best friend, the legendary editor Manuela Pavesi, as interim creative directors. I'd be working directly with Manuela and Jil's design team at the company's HQ in Hamburg, as well as working on the visual campaigns with Jil Sander's art directors, the French duo M+M Paris. The brand was known for sharp, simple, elemental, minimalist tailoring, but there was always a lot of thought behind each of those pared-down pieces. I'd come in with treasures from Portobello Market or the Puces de Clignancourt or the vintage couture boutique Didier Ludot in Paris, and pull them apart for the fabric or embellishments that I thought would complement the collection. I'd also give my advice on fabric buys and develop the colours and textures for the season – a different sleeve, lose the cuff, adapt the cocoon-back of a shirt. In this kind of role, a stylist could kickstart an entire collection with one of their ideas. And then I'd style the runway shows, which took place at Milan Fashion Week.

Not long after I got the job at Jil Sander, my mother had a stroke. She was visiting home in Ghana, and her high blood pressure plus a lifetime of taking care of everyone and everything caught up with her. I got the call from Luther, and I immediately sent her a plane ticket home to London, and got her a place at the private Wellington Hospital, while my father dropped everything to care for her. She was paralysed on her left side, and from then on would have difficulty speaking. I was overwhelmed with dread that the stroke would kill her prematurely, but I was at this point so alienated from my family, and running at such full steam in the fashion world that even if I was logistically helping out, I stayed busy and didn't really let myself feel it. I visited her when I could, though I was still making a lot of excuses for not finding the time, and I introduced her to Uwe.

And then Uwe and I broke up. Given where I stood with the people who had raised me, he had become the closest thing I had to family. And then he was gone too.

So I found myself adrift on a sea of ceaseless work, of late nights and easy laughter, in perpetual and unthinking forward motion. In truth, I was soul-sick, but it would have been unthinkable for me to pause for long enough to ask why. I had nothing and no one to hold me back. I was on a path of self-destruction. At its best, fashion is all about truth, but it can also be a brilliant place to hide. These two states are not mutually exclusive.

Lee McQueen and I had circled each other professionally back when I was still full time at *i-D*. I reviewed one of his Alexander McQueen collections in the magazine in the early 1990s and accused him of racism, and he was so upset over it, he showed up at the magazine and waited downstairs for me for hours to plead his case. I didn't want to hear it, but a while later I ran into him out at a club and before too long we were laughing and drinking and having a ball. So when my relationship with Uwe fell to pieces, and my mother was suffering, I desperately needed a friend, and turned to Lee. He felt like home too: working class like me, and similarly obsessed with cultural arcana and references and research. He was bawdy and cheeky and laughed loudly, the perfect cure for my moroseness. He was devilish and up for a good time whenever I happened to be around. Lee was also one of the most talented designers of his time, capable of transforming women's bodies with his incredibly precise tailoring, while letting his imagination run wild. He passionately loved, and designed for, the fiercest women – the same fuel that fed my fire – indulging their wildest sides and revelling in their fury. He had a dangerous imagination but as a friend, he was simply a comfort.

Along with Lee, my London crew at the time was Guido Palau, a hair stylist working alongside Pat for Steven Meisel, Roland Mouret, who had become a successful fashion designer, and the milliner Philip Treacy. Together we would haunt the Shadow Lounge in Soho. Intimate and chichi, it was dimly lit from below with richly coloured neon, so it felt like a dark jewel box. There was a small sunken dancefloor surrounded by booths, where they played house and disco. Perfect for people-watching or cruising, depending on your mood. It was the kind of place Grace Jones would visit when she was in town, or Naomi. Lee, who loved to dance, ruled it.

Along with carousing, I filled my time up with as much work as I could get my hands on, to escape from the depression I never properly addressed. It would strike in the middle of the night, when my mind would go round and round with self-recrimination: *I'm not being a good son to my mother; I'm turning my back on my family; I'm getting by on charm; did that exasperated look from that photographer mean my work isn't as good as I thought it was?* And on and on and on. I had recurring nightmares where I'd be back home at my parents' flat, and my father would be lecturing me, saying, 'See, I knew you wouldn't last.' I had some truly close friendships, ones that could, alas, be hard to nurture with everyone's schedules, but there were a lot of phony people breezing in and out of my life because I was so deeply afraid to be alone. Increasingly surrounded by too many disingenuous, transitory people, circumstances conspired to make me feel like even more of a fraud.

And then there was the real kicker. Even if my internal monologue was the most ungenerous interpretation, some of what I'd torture myself about was fundamentally true — indeed, I wasn't showing up for the most important people in my life like I should have been. But did that make me a monster? Or someone who was just confused and hurt and running? Some of my panic was also unnecessary pressure I would force upon myself. Like second-guessing my work. I became my own worst critic. The proof was everywhere that my work was actually very good, even if my life was a mess. In fact it was so good that I had started to think maybe my personal chaos was part of the formula for my success. The mess created the tornado that produced the vision. Later in my life I'd see it very differently. But at this stage in my development, since I was on a continuous upward trajectory at work, and work was supposedly the proof that I was doing OK, I had less of an incentive to make real, lasting change in my relationship to myself or others.

One day, around this time, in a blur after my breakup with Uwe and my mother's stroke, my phone rang. It was Naomi calling from Italy. 'I'm with Stefano and Domenico,' she said of the designers of Dolce & Gabbana. 'They love your work. I've just been talking about you and told them we were friends and they want to meet you.' Off I went. Goodbye heartache, hello Milan.

If there is a polar opposite in fashion to Calvin Klein, it might just be Dolce & Gabbana. Where Calvin's output was spare, their clothes were proudly sexualised, highly adorned, occasionally loud, and unapologetically va-va-voom. In thrall to the Italian neorealist cinema of the 1960s, there was always a narrative to their brightly coloured, over-the-top ads, which were mostly shot by Steven Meisel.

Domenico and Stefano held court at their enormous offices in Milan in a salon with two large red thrones. Subtle! Where Domenico was soft-spoken and warm, Stefano was gregarious and sharp. He cracked jokes constantly, loudly, an assistant struggling to keep up translating his highly engaging but 85 per cent Italian monologue. We clicked instantly. They were looking for someone to work with on their menswear and wanted to know what I thought. I told them they needed to lean even harder into their Italianness and sex appeal.

I ended up getting the consulting job, and immediately I had half the runway walking shirtless. (Styling those collections late into the night, Stefano and I could be so loud, Domenico would often yell at us to shut up.) In bringing them ideas for the men's collections the rest of the year, I got them to streamline the clothes, defining things more sharply, making gestures more intentional, though never overstated. With menswear you get to the essence a lot faster. Less hair, fewer makeup tricks, fewer layers. Get to the point. Even if it wasn't my passion as a stylist, I loved working with Stefano and Domenico, who were on a thrilling creative and business high.

Part of my contract included styling the men's ads with Steven Meisel, a proposition that made me delirious. Though his masterful, narrative style is entirely his own, when it comes to fashion imagery, Steven is on a level with such photographic legends as Richard Avedon and Irving Penn. All fashion photographers working today bow down and give Steven his due. As well as a technical perfectionist, he's a complete polymath who could, if he had to, do the models' hair and makeup and style as well as anyone he could hire for himself. But he could and did always hire the very best, including Pat, who was becoming a crucial right hand at his shoots.

Steven liked to work with familiars and so he wasn't keen on the idea of using me for Dolce & Gabbana, but Domenico and Stefano insisted. Before I showed up for the first time on one of his sets, I asked Pat for tips. 'Never take your eyes off the model,' she told me. 'Don't let your gaze stray for an instant. Bring an extra assistant, and always touch the clothes. Encourage him if he gives you ideas: they're likely going to be better than anything anyone else can come up with, anyway. And Edward, he's shy, like you.'

The first shoot I did with Steven was at Pier 59 in New York on the biggest set I'd ever seen. Pat was there, and Guido and Raul Martinez, the art director. I didn't know how Steven would react to me, but when he showed up shortly after, in his hoodie with his horn-rimmed glasses on, I saw immediately that Pat was right. He was shy and quiet, not frosty or aloof. I just said, 'Hi, Steven,' and we got to work. There were no shenanigans on set, the focus was intense – just Steven and the models when he was behind the camera. I was in the presence of God and discovered that with everyone there giving their all, always, so as not to disappoint him, he was actually profoundly nice. Still, I was nervous as hell. He was and remains an undisputed master of my industry. I kept my focus, and in the twenty years since that first shoot I worked on with him, I've never let it go. I still show up to a shoot with Steven as if it were the first time, on my toes. It was known that Steven tried people out on advertising shoots first, and if it worked out, he'd bring them onto the editorial shoots and covers he was doing for *Vogue* Italia. That became my goal.

Amidst this whirlwind, I did sense something I can only describe as a guardian angel, a presence that would occasionally whisper things in my ear that made good sense. As hundreds of thousands of pounds were passing in and out of my bank account, I woke up one day and said to myself, 'You need to buy a house.' It's a very African thing to invest in bricks and mortar. More than anything, you want the permanency and solidity of a tangible, useful asset like a roof over your head. I didn't want to end up like Judy, who had an incredible body of work and no financial security. So I went around to a bunch of local estate agencies in Ladbroke Grove and started looking at flats. I ended up with a perfect-seeming Victorian place on St Michael's Gardens, overlooking a church, a block away from the tiny bedsit apartment I shared with a stylist friend right after moving out of Judy's. I spent a year and a half renovating this new flat, painting it all white, installing oak floors from Switzerland and a pretty, simple, sunny kitchen where I would never cook a single meal. In the meantime, I needed somewhere to park myself when I was in town, so I rented a basement flat on Talbot Road.

And sure, I threw a few parties. Just a few. One of them turned out to be truly auspicious. Some friends finally brought this guy around they had been telling me about. He was interning for the London designer Amanda Wakeley while on a placement year from Northumbria University in Newcastle. My friends knew I always preferred working-class boys, and told me he was handsome in just the way I liked, with chipped teeth and a shaved head. More importantly, he was meant to be really sweet. Lee and Guido and Juergen were there that night, and we were all drinking and getting loud when finally I looked over to my couch and saw Alec for the first time. I felt something move in me. Something I can't adequately describe, even now. It was as if the second hand had stopped ticking, as if there was a tear in the normal space-time continuum. I walked over to him, knelt down, put my hand on his knee and asked, 'Are you gay?' Yes. I was that obvious.

Thankfully, he seemed happy enough to engage. He smiled, I smiled, and suddenly, we were out in the garden talking and drinking beer, surrounded by people who had come outside to smoke. He was soft-spoken and gentle, with a clear, direct way of expressing himself. There was an old soul shining out of him even if he was still in his early twenties. He was the only one I wanted to talk to that night. It felt like I'd already known him for ever. We snuck out of my party and went back to the flat where he was staying with a friend of his family's. The next morning, after we went for breakfast on Old Compton Street, he walked me back home. Inside it was as if a bomb had gone off in my flat. I guess people must have let themselves out at some point in the night.

I knew I was smitten by Alec, but I also knew he had to go back to uni. We saw each other over the few months while he was still on his work placement in town. I'd take him out to dinner someplace of the moment and then he'd insist on reciprocating. With his internship budget, that meant McDonald's or the buffet at Pizza Hut, where we'd spend hours eating slices and talking and laughing. I felt so good just being with him. Where I was dizzy, my attention running all over the place, he was like a solid, straight line. And then he was gone, back to Newcastle. We stayed somewhat lamely in touch, and tried to visit each other for the next year. Mostly I just tried to swallow how much I missed him and then we got into a huge fight over something so stupid and trivial I can't even remember what it was, and so I just did my best to put him out of my mind. Alec felt like home to me. He was a sweet shelter. And then we blew it up.

That meant turning again to work, which was always churning, and always a successful escape. Another ad campaign, another night out, another party back at mine, except this time there'd be no Alec on my couch.

With all this activity, my accounts were in a complete mess. When you work as a stylist, a lot of money passes through your hands. You cover a lot of expenses when producing a mega shoot, some of them massive, and then the client pays you back after you present all your receipts. That only works if you keep your accounts straight, and was I in the kind of shape to do that? Not even remotely. Plus all your receivables pass through your agency, so you need to stay on top of them too to make sure you get paid. There were taxes, which, when you're starting to finally earn, can become their own monster. And I was still sending money home to my parents. It was a completely normal thing to do, especially for an immigrant made good, but it added another spinning plate to the dozens I had going at the same time. My sister Mina helped me stay on top of the bare minimum, but all the brown envelopes from the HMRC were routinely left unopened.

Soon I heard I was being audited for unpaid tax – unsurprising given my total neglect of every detail around me. Except Mina was getting ready to move back to Ghana. She suggested we get our little sister Akua on it, who had got an accounting degree while I was out seeking my fortune. But I had to ask her first, and Akua was proud, fierce and pissed off at me for having made myself so scarce. Whenever I went home to see my mum, she gave me the silent treatment. And when I approached her to come save me from going under, at first it was one-word answers. We were so close growing up, and she was just eleven when I left with no explanation, as far as she was concerned. I was able to endure her side-eye and convinced her to restructure my financial life. Because of the tax drama, even though I never stopped earning, I was in danger of losing my flat, or having to declare bankruptcy. Things had become messy.

I left my finances in her very capable hands and opened more wine. I was having yet another party at home – who knew how much longer I'd have it? – on the night before I was due to arrive in Milan to prepare for Dolce & Gabbana's next show. Finally, I reached my limit. This time, among the group of randoms who had showed up at mine after the club was someone with particularly sticky fingers. I woke up with my head pounding to discover my passport was gone. I panicked and went to the embassy with a bottle of vodka in my pocket. I cannot imagine how I must have looked. (Or smelled.) They told me it would take three days to get the required papers to travel to Milan. I called Domenico and Stefano, begging their forgiveness. Domenico would have to do the first two days of prep without me. I don't think I'd ever felt quite so pathetic in my life.

It was one thing to have personal relationships crash and burn, or not get quite off the ground because I was there but not there. I was used to feeling alone in a room full of people, and there was always someone new around the corner I could charm. Somehow, I had learned to live with the painful guilt over cutting my family loose. But now my bullshit was getting in the way of work, and that was unforgivable in my eyes – a bridge too far.

In the two days while I waited for my paperwork to come together, in between the furious lectures I gave myself, I decided it was time to go cold turkey. I called Pat and told her I was giving up the drink and partying. I had crossed a line, and I was starting to truly hate myself. 'Oh thank God,' she said. Even if I always more or less held myself together, and people who didn't know me as well as Pat did might never have suspected I had a real problem, I could be honest with her. Finally, it was time to be honest with myself too.

STEVEN

New York, 2014.
Steven Meisel taking my picture on a night out.

CHAPTER
SIX

Stepping off the plane at Malpensa, I perceived Milan as a city that had somehow fundamentally changed. Or was it just me who was different? Sometimes fear can be a positive thing. I had scared myself straight.

I was sober, having gone cold turkey and stopped everything but cigarettes. This was the beginning of a six-month period of hiding out from everyone and everything outside of work, because I had such a hard time not going along with the group. If I wasn't on a set or in a library doing research, I was back at my flat or whatever hotel the client had put me up in, watching terrible TV or reading, and not answering the phone. Calls from Kate. Calls from Lee. Calls from Guido. I avoided them all, as the only way I could get sober and stay sober was to simply disappear.

I was quieter, sharper, more focused, even if I was basically white-knuckling to get through it. Akua, who had helped me through the terrifying passport panic so I could finally show up for Dolce & Gabbana, was pleased to see my habitually massive minibar bills reduced to bottled water. (I imagine the clients were pretty thrilled too.) As for me, I was pleased to wake up with a clear head.

While I had minimised my personal affairs down to working, sleeping and eating, Akua continued to make great inroads into my financial ones. Like Luther, she loved fashion, and understood photography and aesthetics, so she could advise me creatively as well as handle my business. It was instantly clear there was one life lesson I desperately needed to learn: not just how to say no to partying, but how to say no to work too. After a decade of hurtling from job to job, it was time to weigh opportunities more coldly. When it came to this, I trusted Akua completely. She could be a fearless bad cop when she needed to be. She put me on tight personal budgets, controlled all my credit cards, and cut out the waste in my life.

Six months into this clear-eyed but somewhat emotionally extreme new chapter, I was getting on a plane to New York City and ran into a stylist friend of mine from back in London. She asked me how I'd been, and when I told her that I'd stopped drinking, and that it was really hard to get my bearings, she told me she was in Alcoholics Anonymous. Back then, in 2004, AA wasn't something I heard talked about so freely in the UK, so I asked her to tell me more. What she relayed made a lightbulb go off in my head. When I got to Manhattan, I found a meeting straight away, and my life turned another corner.

AA encourages you to look at yourself from all sides, to see how the coping mechanisms you have built up over a lifetime are intertwined with your disease. It's not just about not using, but understanding why you do it, and working on how to change those internal processes. Even if years later I'd come to realise I didn't fit the clinical definition of an alcoholic, AA brought me closer to myself in ways that changed me for ever. Apart from coming out of the closet, I'd never really stepped back and taken a full look at myself. Too busy and too fearful to self-examine at an existential level, I had never properly analysed how I operated in my relationships at work, at home, or out in

New York City, late 1990s.
With Pat and Judy Blame
at one of Kate and Naomi's
Halloween parties

London, early 2000s.
With Pat McGrath, Akua
in the background

New York City, 2005. Dolce & Gabbana men's fall-winter campaign, my second with Steven Meisel

London, 2003. Linda
Evangelista recreating early
1990s grunge for *Vogue* Italia

New York City, 2006.
Annabelle Neilson and Lee
McQueen at the Met Gala

Paris, 2014. With Franca
Sozzani at the *Vogue* and
Vanity Fair dinner

Los Angeles, 2008. Naomi
Campbell, one of four covers
for *Vogue* Italia's July 2008
'Black Issue'

New York City, 2005.
Linda Evangelista at the
St. Regis Hotel in 'Makeover
Madness' for *Vogue* Italia's
July 2005 issue

...TOGRAPHED BY STEVEN MEISEL

New York City, 2017. A still
from the 'Bridging the Gap'
campaign for the Gap,
which I directed

New York City, 2011.
With Grace Coddington

London, 2016. Being named a member of the Order of the British Empire for services to diversity in fashion by Anne, Princess Royal

London, 2016. With Madonna at Mark's, the afterparty for my OBE

London, 2016. Outside Buckingham Palace at my OBE Investiture with Alec and his mother Enid, Akua, my father and Naomi

London, 2014. With Rihanna
and Naomi at the British
Fashion Awards, the night I
was given the Isabella Blow
Award for a Fashion Creator

Washington, DC, 2014. With
First Lady Michelle Obama for
the Reach Higher campaign

New York City, 2016. Kate
Moss on a jumbotron in Times
Square as part of the *Seven
Deadly Sins of Edward Enninful*,
directed by Nick Knight

New York City, 2016. Rihanna on
the September 2016 cover of *W*

Paris, 2020. With Virgil
Abloh before his fashion
show for Louis Vuitton men's

London, 2017. Adwoa Aboah
on the December 2017 issue
of British *Vogue*, my first

New York City, 2018. Left
to right: Vittoria Ceretti,
Adut Akech, Faretta, Paloma
Elsesser, Radhika Nair, Yoon
Young Bae, Fran Summers,
Selena Forrest on the May
2018 cover of British *Vogue*

London, 2020. Midwife Rachel
Millar on one of three July
2020 covers of British *Vogue*
celebrating frontline workers
during the pandemic

London, 2022. Left to right, top to bottom: Amar Akway, Majesty Amare, Akon Changkou, Nyagua Ruea, Abény Nhial, Maty Fall, Janet Jumbo, Adut Akech, Anok Yai

London, 2020. Marcus Rashford and Adwoa Aboah on the front cover of British *Vogue*'s September 2020 issue

TIME

Fashioning Change

British *Vogue*'s
Edward Enninful shows
the power of inclusion
BY DIANA EVANS

Paris, 2019. With Oprah
Winfrey at the Stella McCartney
fall-winter 2019 show

September 21, 2020

the world. Through AA meetings and in the daily conversations with my sponsor, I began to understand how I managed (or didn't manage) all the insecurity, anger, rootlessness and fear that I'd internalised. How my ceaseless search for escape, be it an eighteen-hour work day, or ordering another bottle, had hurt me and the people around me. Suddenly, I could see so clearly how I'd touch down in someone's life, whether a new friend, a fling or a fun model I was collaborating with, make them think they were the centre of my world, and then, poof!, I'd disappear in a cloud of smoke. Off to the next fresh face, never letting anyone in, never allowing people the chance to know me beyond the little bit I felt comfortable showing.

I'd never opened myself up like I did to those rooms full of strangers in AA meetings, even if I was still one of the quiet ones. Although sometimes they weren't all strangers. Anonymity is a ground rule in AA, so I won't name anyone here, but I reunited with a lot of friends from work whom I had assumed had just fallen off the face of the earth. No, they were in recovery too, and they would become another layer of support.

It was hard enough to talk about my worst fears even with people I was close to – emotional display is not a prized quality in Ghanaian households. Yet, for the first time in my life, I was starting to see the power in it. People say confession is an unburdening, and it's true. When you are an addict who gets sober, every fear you buried along the way comes raging to the surface. In those months, I felt a rush of isolation, loneliness, impostor syndrome, the ongoing and ever-present pain of racism, and that aching hurt from feeling cut off from my family. It's hard to overstate what it meant for me to finally unburden myself.

The spiritual side of AA was absolutely fine with me, I've always believed in God and guardian angels, so it wasn't so hard to put faith in a power greater than myself. As I continued to go to meetings regularly, I started to become a sponsor myself, helping others just as others had helped me. The anonymity of AA allows the distances between people from all walks of life to shrink. Inside a meeting, there are no worldly trappings, no status signifiers that make someone's experience count more than anyone else's. It's not that fashion was some toxic place I needed to escape – there were plenty of people full of love and loyalty. But to me, AA was a balm, a leveller and a welcome reminder that a person's world does not begin and end with whether or not they shot the Prada campaign that season.

I stayed fourteen years in the programme, after which I felt like I had enough of a handle on my consumption, and myself, to be able to sip a little tequila every now and again without bringing on a crisis. Many people in the programme can't do that, and when I realised I could is when I changed the way I identified myself. Nevertheless I needed structure and rigour, and the twelve steps were there for me. They were a plan of action, a checklist for the way forward, that sorted me out and helped me develop conscious accountability to others. As part of the all-important ninth step, making amends to friends and family, I told my mother how sorry I was for all the times

I avoided her. 'Don't be silly,' she said to me. 'I'm your mother, you don't have to apologise.' (My mother was always hardwired for forgiveness.) I told the same thing to my siblings too, who just teased me about it. 'What are you talking about?' they'd laugh, but I knew how I felt. I didn't reach out to my father. That was still one step too far. But I did reach out to Uwe, who became a real friend. And I reached out to Alec.

It was a year to the day since we had last been in touch when I sent him an email. I told him I wanted to mark the anniversary, and let him know there were no hard feelings about how we left things. If he ever wanted to get together and talk, I was happy to. Alec was backpacking around Australia on his own – he couldn't have been further away physically – but he replied right away. He told me he had four more weeks on his trip, and from then on we started emailing every day, catching each other up on our lives, telling each other how much we looked forward to reconnecting.

When we saw each other again in London upon his return, we both knew we were ready. Alec loved that I'd got sober. He found me changed. There was less noise and fewer people around us now, unlike the snowballing twenty-four-hour party that used to trail me wherever I went. We spent a lot of nights at home in my now-finished flat in Ladbroke Grove. We would light candles and buy flowers. One night I wanted to make a show of domesticity and make him a home-cooked meal. Naturally, physically cooking anything myself was completely out of the question. To this day I still can't really decipher the switches on my oven, which appear to resemble the control panel on an aeroplane, so I ordered in some homey-looking fare from a local restaurant and passed it off as my own. A few months later, I made the mistake of ordering exactly the same food as takeaway. Alec twigged immediately, and then told me on the night I'd been merrily passing myself off as a domestic goddess, he'd already seen the plastic takeaway boxes in the bin, anyway. But that's how love goes, isn't it? He knew I could barely open a packet of crisps. He was just flattered that I was trying to impress him.

Alec was never much of a drinker and decided right away to become sober alongside me. It wasn't a requirement. My problem with self-control was my own; he could do whatever he wanted to, drink or not drink, as long as he was happy and healthy. I said it so often he started to get annoyed, as his willingness to join me in that project was a gesture of friendship and love. But then I have always known Alec to be kind, steady and conscientious; he is rooted to the ground where I float above it.

Alec put in long days because he was ambitious too, and as a working-class kid like me, he had no reason to expect that life would simply hand him his dreams. As we spent more time together, with him more or less moving into my flat, I saw how our work ethics matched. We'd spend so much time sitting in the living room together, each of us working in our separate corners, every now and again one of us waving the other over to ask an opinion or share a creative solution that felt like a victory. He understood my work and had a great eye, and I supported what he did and believed in it, and lent him my opinions whenever he asked. We turned into each other's own best editors.

We got a car together, a convertible BMW, a big one, and would drive around London with the top down as if we were in California, never mind that it was freezing cold half the time. We'd get excited by the same gallery shows and shops, and it was like an avalanche of shared interests and inspiration. We were building a real life together as proper partners.

Alec was designing full time and lecturing often, but he was falling more deeply in love with filmmaking. New York was a better place to develop that as a proper career than London, and as I needed to spend more time there too, off we went to New York together. It was out of the question that we'd be apart. The London flat would be there for us whenever we wanted to come back, which was still pretty often.

Meanwhile, Steven Meisel had got in touch with my agent to see if I'd style an ad campaign he was shooting for Valentino. Apparently, I had passed the test on his set for Dolce & Gabbana men's. Then – cue the harps and singing angels – Valentino went so well that I got the call I had been pining for: to style a feature for him for *Vogue* Italia. This was it: collaborating with the master on his ultimate canvas. It was going to be Gothic, my agent said – lots of black – and it was going to be in Los Angeles, where Steven had moved. It was for the March 2004 cover, with multiple fashion pages inside.

Working with Steven on ad campaigns, where the client has a lot of input, is one thing. Working with Steven on an editorial shoot, where he has carte blanche to do whatever he wants, is something else entirely. Pat briefed me: you need to bring an enormous amount of clothes, because he might get an inspiration in the middle of the shoot and want to go in a different direction. 'What's that, Steven? You're thinking 1940s? OK, I've got something.' Or 'Oh now you want 1950s?' God help me if I didn't know the difference. For Steven, stylists will get unique pieces made, custom shoes designed. They'll stock up on hats, furs, gloves, cuffs, anklets, you name it. He's an accessories monster with an endless appetite for new combinations, and you want to be ready and you want to please him. When Guido worked with him, he'd bring cases and cases of wigs in every shape, every shade, adaptable to any era, that cost tens of thousands of dollars, because it was Steven, and for Steven we do our utmost to ensure he can reach that pitch of highly expressive beauty that only he can create.

So I went all-in on the clothes prep for this shoot. Alas, the same couldn't be said for the new assistant I hired, who failed to fill out the paperwork correctly for the shipment after I had gone on ahead to LA. Everything got held up in customs. Disaster. I spent my first prep day in town racing around Melrose Avenue trying to come up with alternatives, while Akua had to drop everything to fly over from London herself with cases and cases. A thrown-together wardrobe would be awful under any circumstance, but for my first shoot with Steven for *Vogue* Italia?

Unthinkable. Thankfully, he got to the set later than the rest of us, so he missed Akua hurriedly wheeling the clothes racks up to the loading area, minutes before he arrived. I had been on an adrenaline high for weeks preparing the shoot. Frankly, this eleventh-hour scramble was too much.

But you push on. I threw on a smile, summoned what calm I could and went over to greet the maestro. Granted, Steven can seem more myth than man to those who never get a glimpse inside his inner orbit, so it's worth pointing out that in person he is one of the smartest, wittiest, most creative and curious men you could wish to meet. Lest we forget, it was the exacting eye of this native New Yorker that enshrined the original supermodels in the public's imagination, that gave us Madonna in all her peroxide power, whose photography crystallised every fashion movement, from glamour to grunge, of the past forty years. Like many geniuses, his work is powered by a fierce and fastidious mono-focus. Collaborating with him is not for the faint-hearted, but he has enormous kindness and ferocious loyalty for those he loves, and a deep respect and patience for anyone who sits for him, be they a teen or a titan. He can also be a real laugh.

We got straight down to the clothes. I started off with simpler looks, like a low-slung trouser, a white shirt with rolled-up sleeves and then another look with pants. Clean, directional, taste level on point. Steven was responsive but by the time he'd seen the third button-down shirt in a row, he rolled his eyes at me and laughed. 'Can't you do anything else?'

Oh, honey. Out came furs, lace, leather, fashion. Steven likes to dress models in a grand way. Think volume, which drives impact and creates a frame-filling composition. The images need to be memorable. From that first editorial, and the countless number we have worked together on since, he has schooled me. He is like a one-man Oxbridge for fashion. Once you have matriculated at Meisel, you are fully formed.

The same is true for new models. Steven was a starmaker, obsessed with introducing girls to the world. He'd work with one or two constantly for a year, teaching them how to pose and move, and they became the centre of his attention. On set, he'd put a full-length mirror next to him, facing the girl, so she could see herself while they both worked. He put the models at ease, always asking if they needed anything. Water? Diet Coke? A cigarette? He instantly recognised and captured their best gestures, the singular things that make them the most unguardedly themselves, which made them feel as beautiful as they looked, so they gave that much more. Even with all the splashier flourishes going on – accessories, colour, Pat's way-out makeup, an elaborate set – Steven could navigate the visual noise and dial into the turn of a cuff, the flick of a wrist, the way Naomi's nose wrinkled when she laughed. And – oh my days – that lighting! No one could match what he can do to make skin luminous.

My shoots then, as now, owe a great deal to the rigour I developed in those years. The power of the original idea is still paramount, but the process of making fashion imagery is like a game of 3D chess. A host of skills are required: charm, hustle and a little ruthlessness to secure exclusive access to a brand's best looks of the season; close relationships with designers to entice the world's greatest to create custom looks for the vision; a sixth sense to cast the ideal model at the perfect moment; a deep knowledge and instant recall of fashion history coupled with the confidence and intuition to shape its future; to say nothing of pitch-perfect support staff. And that's just what's needed before you've even arrived on set.

On shoot days, my MO became to leave no eventuality unaccounted for. There are OK shoots, great shoots and utterly sublime ones but, in essence, the aim is always the same: to bottle stardust. For me, the core of the mission has remained unchanged: to make the woman in front of the camera feel alive, confident, fearless and utterly true to herself. If she feels like the ideal version of herself, it's a better time for everyone, and it'll also get the best results. Though I arrive with a series of final looks meticulously planned for the camera, I also create an Ali Baba's cave of possibilities. Table upon table are neatly laid out with every colour and length of glove or style of hat, bag or heel, and rack after rack contain the most enticing pieces of the season, punctuated by a dash of vintage, while a line of security guards keeps an eye on the fine jewellery.

All this extra preparation gives us the flexibility to play with all sorts of characters, while making the subject feel like the most adored person in the world. Whether it's 7 a.m. in rainy North London and I'm watching a bleary-eyed Taylor Swift light up at the fashion fantasia I've laid out for her, or I'm in Los Angeles after dark with a cast of twenty models round a pool, the mood on set is everything. Whether the subject is a pop star or politician, activist or supermodel, there is no retouching, no dress of the season, that will ever make someone look better than when they are truly feeling themselves from within.

That first story with Steven in LA started a string of collaborations that has continued to this day, with many of them becoming touchstones in fashion history. Twice a year, Franca would give over most of the magazine to Steven. We had only five days to shoot the eighty-page 'Makeover Madness' story for the July 2005 issue. In it, Linda Evangelista led a pack of models getting transformed by plastic surgeons on sets that resembled an uptown doctor's surgery and a medi-spa. It was savage and controversial to show the underbelly of what so many do to compete in the game of beauty. This was the era when cosmetic procedures, treatments and 'tweakments' were no longer the preserve of Upper East Side ladies in hush-hush doctors' waiting rooms. Suddenly, it seemed everyone was having a little something done. It's just that the bruises and bandages weren't what anyone was supposed to see, much less style, light and turn into a fashion narrative. We pushed it. We showed bruised women wearing expressions of pain, their faces and bodies marked up for the knife, all to serve the modern diktat to 'look their best'. I loved the way Steven inserted himself into the moment, often in a critical way. He didn't want just to reflect the world, but to twist it.

My taste for bringing reality into fashion was refined by his deliriously surreal eye, and before long we'd find our shoot subjects in op-ed pieces in newspapers from New York to London. Together we did girls gone wild in the supermarket, heiresses at the laundromat, an ode to poor Britney Spears, whose public meltdown at the time had occasioned a paparazzi swarm that both fascinated and enraged us. We even did an editorial composed entirely from primitive chat-room screen-grabs, an ode to a world where people were just starting to stream themselves online.

You'd work out an idea with Steven, a character, a setting, and since he could do it all, there were truly no limits. As this was before anyone in fashion was using the internet for visual research, I started spending all my downtime when I was back in London at the *Vogue* library, in the basement of the building I now work in in Hanover Square, where all the international editions had bound volumes, one for each year, in some cases going over a century. Or I'd go to the reference library at Central Saint Martins. I bought books constantly, the more random the better: on 1950s land sculpture, or the Old West, or nineteenth-century ideas about ghosts. I still loved street fashion, but Steven added so many narrative and aesthetic layers that I had completely left grunge behind.

Steven's standards are so high that even if he was good-humoured with me, I felt like I was fucking up all the time. We'd be doing a story with swimsuits and I'd pull out some dayglo thing with a cutout and he'd look at it and laugh, 'That's the tackiest thing I've ever seen.' Any time I couldn't make him love something, I'd have to just go back and find something chicer. There were times during the three years when we were collaborating most intensely that I felt like I really didn't have a life. But it kept me in line. I didn't want to drink, because I had another shoot with Steven, and I had to bring my best every time. It was exhausting, but because of the focus he required, I kept myself together, my relationship together, and moved onto a higher professional plane all at the same time.

The world was noticing. More designers started reaching out for me to consult and style their advertising campaigns and runway shows: Giorgio Armani, Fendi, Valentino, Lanvin, Sonia Rykiel, my beloved Comme des Garçons. I was starting to rack up covers on multiple international *Vogue* editions in the same month and was still doing my job for *i-D*. The next logical step would be a call from American *Vogue*, who had a roster of contributing editor stylists on board. But for some reason, that call didn't come.

It didn't come and didn't come and didn't come, and as the months ticked by, I started to feel overlooked; a massive trigger that played right into my old insecurities. I was learning to engage with rather than bury and numb my anger at moments like these. 'Steven, your friend Grace Coddington hates me,' I'd say of *Vogue*'s creative director, who was then Anna Wintour's most trusted and brilliant fashion lieutenant, a flame-haired Brit and one-time *Vogue* cover model, an industry legend who was inarguably the greatest stylist working.

He'd reply, 'That's weird because she's always telling me she loves your work.'

'Pffft, are you for real?' I cried. Grace's approval meant *everything*; her eye was the best in the business. I was doing very well, more prolific than ever, helping change the conversation. So where was the call?

And then in 2005, as I was eating an ice cream in Midtown with one of my best friends, bitching about how fucked the industry was and why didn't Grace call, in mid-rant, the phone rang. It was her. (It was actually kind of spooky.) 'Edward, I'd love you to come in and meet Anna,' she said. Camilla Nickerson, who had been working in *Vogue*'s fashion department with Grace, was leaving for *W*, thereby setting the fashion merry-go-round in motion and opening up a rare spot on American *Vogue*'s elite roster. For a second, I thought it was a prank call. I was ecstatic. I called Steven; I called Pat; I called Naomi, who started crying. And then I pulled myself back down to Earth. I gave myself a stern talking-to, like a would-be Oscar nominee, my hands yet to grasp the statuette. *You probably won't get it*, I'd say to myself. *But it's an honour just to be nominated.* Grace had asked me to come in the following day. The morning of the interview, I changed four times, discarding black suit after black suit till I found the right one.

OK, since you know you won't get this, I told myself in the cab on the way to *Vogue*'s office in Times Square, *just try to have fun when you go in. Then it won't be a total loss.* So as I glided up in the elevator, through the glass doors, past the racks of clothes and walls of iconic photographs by Avedon and Irving Penn, I was in pretty good spirits. Grace led me into Anna Wintour's sun-strewn corner office and introduced us. There she was, her arms folded, her bob impeccable. I handed her my book and as she leafed through it, we got to talking about London. 'How's Portobello?' That kind of thing. This went on for a few minutes until she looked up from the pages and asked, 'So are there any photographers you *haven't* worked with yet?' I thought of the images I had just walked past and said, 'They're all dead.' She laughed, as if to say, *Who is this nut?* But I felt no need to walk on eggshells. The interview was a success.

Yet the days passed and I heard nothing. On set with Steven and Pat the following week they started teasing me about how I must have really blown it. I'd found out from one of them that two very hot stylists whose work I really respected were also interviewing. I just figured, OK, they're white; it's over. *Vogue* is for trust-fund girls, not for me. André Leon Talley was the only person of colour working at the magazine then. He was a glorious anomaly, but an anomaly just the same. I shrugged it off. But then, just as I was whipping through the racks to get another look together, I got a call from Grace. 'Edward, we'd love for you to come and join us.' I hung up and screamed, 'I got it!'

'That's the last one I'll ever train!' Steven shouted back. He knew the demands of this job would mean we'd work together less, so in a way, he was losing me. At *Vogue*, I'd need to be in the office two weeks a month, pitching ideas and putting clothes together and getting them past Anna, and then I'd spend the other two weeks working on commercial jobs for money. It meant collaborating with whichever photographer Anna chose. And it meant taking into account the business side of the fashion industry, which was an element of my education that I was keen to improve.

American *Vogue* is a different animal from the international editions. Under Anna's tenure, the magazine transcended its role as straightforward media outlet to become an important fashion power broker. American *Vogue* does not celebrate creativity for creativity's sake; it tries to balance art and commerce. Just as Steven moulds stylists, Anna does too, but in a way that's very geared towards their impact on the industry's bottom line. American *Vogue* moves product and validates designers like almost nothing else. If one of the dresses you pull ends up running in the magazine, it's going to have a markedly different fate than if it doesn't make the cut, which is why Anna and the fashion staff are rigorous about their curation. And the stories are generally shorter than Steven's at *Vogue* Italia, so there's more pressure on each item, and on each idea.

Of course, everyone is always fascinated by Anna. She's unsentimental, but if she respects you, she listens to you. From Anna I'd learn how to intuit the mainstream from an editorial standpoint, as opposed to working to fulfil the agenda of a single designer, as I did as a consultant. You couldn't do stories that were too out-there, or they'd end up in the bin. Stories had to be safe but not too boring. Walking that very fine line was hard to learn. I didn't suffer too many personal casualties, thankfully, though there was one colour-block story that I shot with the photographers Inez van Lamsweerde and Vinoodh Matadin in the Hamptons about a year after I started that met a sticky end. Unbeknownst to me, Anna killed the story and Grace reshot it with a different photographer. The amusing twist in the tale was that it was all captured in the documentary *The September Issue*, whose crew had been shadowing *Vogue* staffers over the course of a few months. You have to laugh: the documentary played on it a bit for the drama, but I had already worked there for a while and knew that getting stories killed or reshot came with the job. It happened to all of us, even legends like Tonne Goodman and Camilla as well, sometimes even Grace. It was more like, when a story you worked on made it into print, you were ecstatic.

At *Vogue* I was no longer rebelling against 'commercial fashion' like some indie-mag kid; I was part of it. I never stopped trying to bring something new, to document the times and make a difference. But despite the huge platform, it was hard not to feel creatively stifled in those years. My journey had been about art, and my work had always resonated best when there was at least some strand running through it that connected to what was happening in society. Here there was some room for that kind of work, but also an ongoing need for simpler, more elemental, less topical fare. Still, I certainly honed my business skills.

Anna had a sort of unofficial list of models she was eager to push and whom we were encouraged to use when we pitched her. There weren't a lot of Black ones, but I rocked the boat. If I wanted a story with eight Black girls, instead of just the usual one, often all I had to do was ask. (Once again, I became known to the staff as 'the guy who shoots Black girls', which was pretty reductive, but fine by me if it at least meant more women of colour in the pages.) Even those 'models go to Africa' stories got another twist. I explained to Anna that the conventional approach of a white woman surrounded by natives was hurtful and offensive, but that didn't mean Africa should be off-limits to a fashion imagination. One fashion story that she commissioned took place in Mali. I cast Liya Kebede, who is from Ethiopia, explaining how important it was to centre African narratives on African women. This is one of many reasons why diverse perspectives are so crucial on a staff. Without varied points of view, at best you're limiting yourself creatively. At worst, you're creating work that belittles, offends and does far more harm than good.

It's no secret that in the past, *Vogue*'s parent company Condé Nast was not an easy place for Black and Brown employees. Throughout the latter years of the twentieth century and early twenty-first century, its stable of magazines was built on a very specific fantasy of money, social privilege, whiteness and thinness, and nowhere was that more apparent than at *Vogue*. Some months, it felt like being a redhead or a brunette rather than a blonde was what counted for diversity.

Unsurprisingly, the staff was overwhelmingly white too, and it was impossible not to feel it.

In the fashion industry at large, things were absolutely dire as well. Black models were disappearing from catwalks. I remember sitting front row one Fashion Week in 2007 with the absence even more glaring than the season before, with runway after runway filled with blonde after blonde after stone-faced blonde. I wasn't the only one to notice. Naomi was up in arms. As was Bethann Hardison, a barrier-breaking model in the 1970s turned agent, whom I used to work with all the time at *i-D*. She represented some of the best Black models in the business, but by now Bethann had given up agenting to fashion a role for herself as an industry-wide oracle and urgent voice for diversity. She was well known and respected, and used her influence fearlessly. She'd call up designers and casting agents who weren't working with women of colour and challenge them. That year, after that shambolic whitewashed season, she held her first town hall in New York – a panel discussion with such notables as Naomi and her best friend Iman. They educated the assembled public and throngs of press on the scourge of 'no Black, no ethnic' casting notices that brands were sending out to model agents. Bethann started keeping public track of the ethnicity of every model in every magazine and show, to quantify what everyone who cared was already aware of. It shouldn't have been radical, but it was. There was a radical need.

I remember talking to Steven about the situation. He grew up in the Bronx, had a lot of Black close friends and was one of those white people who got it. 'Let's do something with Franca,' he said. She was present at Bethann's first panel discussion and agreed the industry needed seismic change. And so was born the idea for the July 2008 edition of *Vogue* Italia, or 'The Black Issue', as it's come to be known. Cover to cover, every shoot, every page, would feature and celebrate Black people. Nothing like it had ever been done before.

A few short months before America would vote Barack Obama into the White House, the issue went on sale, and promptly sold out its original print run in three days. Unheard of. It went into multiple reprints – unprecedented for a monthly magazine that wasn't commemorating a mass global tragedy. The lion's share of the credit for that issue is down to Steven and his tireless agent Jimmy Moffat, and Franca. I styled the cover of Naomi and played a central role, too. Among the stories I did inside, one featured the stunning plus-size model Toccara Jones, dripping with diamonds, heaving with cleavage, on a motorcycle, over twelve pages. (Plus-size models are still too rare on fashion sets, but in 2008, it was much, much worse.)

With this issue, we presented so many different kinds of Black beauty, so many out-there chic ideas that it should have made it impossible to pigeonhole Black people for evermore. (If only, right?) If the excitement around it was immense, it was also bittersweet, because it came under the guise of a 'special' issue. Doubtless, it was a professional peak, and I still hear from people today how much that issue meant to them. But I remember thinking to myself that things would only change when we had Black women in magazines every month, in multiple stories, with multiple points of view and styles and looks. This became my goal. I repeated it like a mantra: 'Get yourself into a position where one day you can make that happen yourself.'

My career was in a good place: my output increased in quantity and prestige, and I was beginning to understand how I could use fashion in new and powerful ways to start important conversations. And yet my sober self was still finding new ways to deal with stress, not all of them good. I have always been a hypochondriac, which I can trace back to all those trips to and from the hospital in Ghana in abject pain when I was little. But during those years when we spent so much time in New York, it went into obsessive overdrive. Not long after Alec and I moved into our apartment in Chelsea, I felt a lump in my neck. I was convinced I had cancer. This happens to most people at some point in their life – they find a weird lump and start mentally catastrophising – but I couldn't let it go. I was fixated on the idea that I was going to die, imminently and painfully. I had tests, I consulted more than one doctor. When multiple clean bills of health couldn't calm me down, I finally admitted the problem was my compulsive negative thinking, which I was no longer masking with partying. I found a hypnotherapist and went to a few sessions to slow down the hamster wheel, and it worked. (The lump was long gone by then.) The reprieve was welcome, but unfortunately, only temporary.

Meanwhile, my weight was going up and down more drastically than ever. The problem was, I ate when I was happy, and hypochondria aside, I was really happy. Despite some of the wider complications, I loved most of my *Vogue* colleagues and being part of the team, and Alec and I were in a honeymoon phase. But all the travel and long hours triggered sickle-cell crises, and with them, reminders of how the world outside the fashion industry still saw me. In Paris during one show season, I had a flare-up so bad that I needed to ask the hotel to help me find a doctor who could make a house call. And when they did, and the doctor arrived at my room at the Ritz, he wouldn't believe the very legitimate reason why I was asking for morphine. He assumed I was a junkie – a *Vogue* editor in a five-star hotel during Fashion Week? – and when I couldn't prove otherwise, he refused to give me the only treatment that would take the pain away. It was the same old racist story, one that even visible success can't protect you from. White doctors often assume Black people can handle more pain, and write off our real agony as histrionics or drug-seeking. It was yet another study in contrasts.

An even worse pain came in February 2010, when Lee McQueen died by suicide. Lee and I had just made up after falling out the year before. We were meant to do a show of his together, and he cancelled at the last minute. After months, I broke down and called him to say I was over it, and that I missed him. We went out for the kind of dinner we used to do all the time: it was me and Alec, Kate, and Mert Alas and Marcus Piggott, a pair of photographers I worked with constantly at *Vogue*. Afterwards, we all went back to Mert and Marcus's place and listened to Diana Ross, Lee's favourite, and danced till morning. And then a few weeks later, I got a call from Mert with the news that Lee had been found dead in his apartment. I burst into loud, angry tears. I couldn't believe the world would go on without him, and that I had lost such a friend.

Our friendship was rooted in celebration and joy. He had incredible intuition; he was one of the best judges of character of everyone I knew. He gave great advice and had a great eye. But we were there to lift each other up, not help each other wallow. That meant that, like so many of his close friends, I wasn't aware how depressed Lee was. I had no idea that his life was in danger. It was a brutal shock. I called Anna to let her know, and then it was endless calls to Kate, to Steven and Pat, to Guido and Naomi, all of us sobbing and bewildered. *What would Lee think of this?* is something I catch myself saying almost daily. And in that way, he's still with me.

Battles raged on. The Black Issue should have killed off the stupid, tired adage that Black girls on covers don't sell magazines, but I continued to hear it all the time, anyway. I had made some progress with my editorials, but I was itching for a bigger platform, one where I could create a vision of the world as I knew it to be: a bolder, more inclusive one.

My wish came true in 2011, when Stefano Tonchi, the artistically minded and cerebral editor-in-chief of *W* magazine, then a Condé Nast stablemate, asked me to be its fashion and style director. In the Condé Nast hierarchy at the time, *W* was in a glorified position: it had the back office and advertising support of the most heavyweight glossy publishing house in the world, but a much freer hand to be edgier and more intellectual. The remit and responsibilities would allow me to deliver the impact I'd had at *i-D*, except on a much bigger stage. (Figuratively and literally. *W* prints in a luxuriously larger scale than most glossies.) The decision was not a difficult one. I wanted this job.

I could sense it wasn't just my CV that needed a shakeup, it was the whole notion of the modern fashion magazine. By 2011, the traditional style bibles had almost entirely stopped featuring models on the cover in favour of smiley celebrities looking as approachable and uncontroversial as possible, while the tabloids and internet recycled the same paparazzi and red-carpet images ad nauseam. Celebrity imagery had become ubiquitous and banal. Stefano, along with *W*'s celebrity editor Lynn Hirschberg and I, decided it was time for a tonal transformation. This has always been one of my specialities – doing unexpected and out-of-the box makeovers – but at *W* it shifted to an entirely new level. Major heavyweight movie stars, wrangled by Lynn, were willing to put themselves into my hands and let me radically overhaul them for the day. They were more than willing, actually. They were delighted, as it was often a huge boon to them too. *W* cover transformations soon became something to look forward to every month.

It was during this time that I met Rihanna. And I was enthralled. Occasionally as a stylist you are lucky enough to meet a creative force who, by some strange, intangible alchemy, brings every ounce of your creativity into focus. We met at a Lanvin show midway into my tenure at *W*, shot together for the first time shortly afterwards, and I've never stopped shooting with her since. When it comes to fashion literacy, Rihanna just gets it. She reminds me of Kate in that way. She understands references, characters and images. And she will never repeat a look from her ever-growing legacy of them, so working with her means pushing for something new every time. I love the challenge, and our work together remains among my favourites in my career.

Stefano had already assembled his team when I started my job, and I was happy to work with them. But at Condé Nast, there was now an opportunity to reach out to Black employees company-wide, through monthly meetings. Part networking, part open discussion, I always attended whenever I was in town. Senior-level colleagues pressed on the younger kids the importance of reaching out for advice and mentoring, and were there as a sounding board. Those of us in positions of authority would take their calls when they needed us, meet them for coffee when we could, and we'd always tell it to them straight. Sometimes they just needed us to listen to their frustrations and comfort their fears. Sometimes they needed us to raise things with human resources. An important moment comes in any successful career when you must begin to raise up the generation behind you. For those of us in under-represented groups, this work is, and remains, especially urgent. We have to look out for, encourage and teach our own.

Meanwhile, the media landscape was churning in an exciting new way. When I was due to start at *W*, which, as head of all the fashion in the magazine, was a higher-profile position than I'd had at *Vogue*, Alec came to me and said, 'You know there's this social network called Twitter, and this brand new one called Instagram. I know you're very bougie these days, but there's a whole world of fashion fans out there and you should communicate with them.' I was always more of a behind-the-scenes person, but *Sure*, I thought. That could be fun. Why not speak to people directly? We signed me up and I posted my very first tweet, the announcement of my new role at *W*. As the followers grew minute by minute, I began to communicate directly with a new generation for the first time. What came back to me blew my mind. There were so many kids out there who knew my work. And who told me that what I was doing was important to them, that I was inspiring them in their careers, helping them project themselves into fashion, reflecting their beauty back to them and giving them new ways to dream.

People talk about Instagram and Twitter as if they are only mindless diversions, or mental health triggers, but the exchanges they fostered for me with younger generations helped me step into a greater sense of mission. I always felt a responsibility to show the world the beauty in diversity, but now for the first time I was seeing how much what I did could uplift these kids in particular. Because I was now communicating in words as well as images through social media, my voice amplified fashion's potential to communicate positively to the world, and how the industry needed to open itself up more. 'If I can do it, with my background and experience, you can too,' became my mantra when kids DM-ed me or responded to my posts. Study, intern, assist people, ask questions, believe in yourself, I would tell them. Walk before you run, don't assume you know more than you do, and respect your elders, but never give up. Fight for your images, fight for respect, reach out for help and support when you need it. I discovered that a lot of people assumed I was the son of some rich Ghanaian who went to Oxford. Hilarious! So through social media, posting old photos and talking about my experiences, I could actually show them and tell them that anything was possible.

I used social media as a way to call people out, too. It proved to be a uniquely effective way to bring attention to when our industry needed to do better. In 2013, covering Haute Couture Week in Paris with the *W* team, I couldn't believe it when two designers tried to seat me, and only me, in the second row, while my white colleagues, all fashion directors like myself, were in front. I'm not at shows to pose for pictures or feed my ego. I'm there to take in every detail of a collection from the best vantage point possible. I'll often see six shows in a day, or more, so every minute counts. Editors go to shows to spark ideas, and you'd think the designers and their PR people would have understood that seating me with the best line of sight possible was in their interest. My whole team was flabbergasted, so I pulled out my phone. *Not today*, I thought, and began to type: 'If all my (white) counterparts are seated in the front row, why should I be expected to take 2nd row? Racism? xoxo.' The tweet made headlines.

Accountability was now a buzzword in the industry, however faint. A few months after that show, Bethann announced a beefed-up organisation she called The Diversity Coalition, launching with an even bigger splash than her 2007 town hall, on the eve of New York Fashion Week in September 2013. Bethann read out an open letter to the governing bodies of the four major Fashion Weeks: New York, London, Milan and Paris, and named each designer who had, in the previous season, featured only one model of colour, or none at all. Big names like Calvin Klein, Rodarte, Proenza Schouler and Louis Vuitton came under the microscope. People listened, and the following season, things got markedly better. Naomi, who is always ready to use the power of her celebrity to say what needs to be said, went on Channel 4 to underline the point. Calvin went from no models of colour to six, she said. This made a difference to everyone.

As my visibility increased, recognition followed, which was a strange feeling, but a satisfying one. In 2014, I got a call from the New York Urban League, an important non-profit geared to creating educational and career opportunities for Black and other underserved communities in New York. Apparently, I was going to receive a Frederick Douglass Award. Bethann had put me up for it. Of all the awards I've received since, this one holds a very dear place in my heart, as it exists to recognise Black excellence. In the room that night were luminaries from business and politics, and then, thanks to Jonathan Newhouse, who bought a table for the ceremony, my group represented fashion. Ronnie Newhouse, Iman, the Black British model Jourdan Dunn, Diane von Furstenberg, Olivier Rousteing from Balmain, Jimmy Moffat and Alec were there, as well as Naomi, who presented me with the award.

Ever the editor, I took advantage of Naomi, Iman and Olivier's presence in New York to put together a shoot at *W*, which we invited Rihanna to join. Three generations of Black fashion icons together, with a promising young Black designer: what's not to love? It was on that shoot, watching Naomi and Rihanna become friends, that I got wind that I was getting another big award, this time the British Fashion Council's Fashion Creator award. It had been named for the brilliantly eccentric tastemaker and fashion muse Isabella Blow, who had passed in 2007, and it celebrated people who were pushing the fashion industry forward. I was really thrilled. Once again, Naomi agreed to present it. (We were starting to make a habit of it.) What I didn't know until I took to the stage at a packed Royal Albert Hall in London months later to accept it, was that Naomi had also got Rihanna to fly herself and her team in to co-present. These goddesses had my back.

I remember standing there backstage just as they were about to call my name, feeling so blessed, so appreciated and recognised. *God, my life is going so well*, I thought to myself. *Too well. Something bad must be about to happen.*

No sooner had this thought finished forming itself in my mind when a piercing ringing noise suddenly shocked its way into my ear.

What was happening? I'd never had good hearing, and decades spent at nightclubs next to giant speakers hadn't helped. Standing in the wings, waiting to go on stage, I panicked. I didn't want to start falling apart. Thoughts are powerful. Had I been too careless with mine? I could just about pick out conversations and ambient noise, but the ringing stayed with me all night: through the beautiful montage film that Alec had made that ran before Naomi and Rihanna's sweet introduction, showing my greatest hits; through the hugs and kisses from well-wishers after the ceremony, when Tom Ford shook my hand and told me how he finally realised just how good my work really was; all through the party afterwards, where practically the entire fashion world was kicking up its heels dancing and patting me on the back.

And there the ringing stayed. Into the next morning, and the next morning, and onwards through every day since. It was hard to escape my age-old fear. That with the good there always comes the bad.

EVERYBODY
RISE

*New York, 2013, Me, André Leon Talley
and Naomi Campbell backstage at DVF.*

CHAPTER
SEVEN

Camilla Nickerson always used to tease me about being a 'church boy', and she wasn't wrong. We're all sinners, a notion that, to me, doesn't have much to do with fire and brimstone, but rather serves as a simple, useful reminder that none of us is perfect, nor beyond reproach. Though my understanding of righteousness differs from the Christian tradition of my upbringing, I have more than just faith in some amorphous higher power: I've felt an unseen, but very real hand guide my life so many times. I believe that doing good is its own reward, but I also believe that moral failings have consequences. On this night in London, and in the years that followed, I would evolve my understanding of morality, and what I understood to be the meaning of fate. Coming through one of the most harrowing trials of my life, I would eventually stop seeing myself as its victim.

At the time, it was my habit that when something bad happened, like my hearing sputtering out on a night when I was receiving an important recognition from the fashion world, I'd turn in on myself. Did I do something to bring on this misfortune? How could this somehow be my fault? The contrasts of that evening weighed heavy on my mind. I saw the good of what I'd built all around me: onscreen in Alec's film montage of my work, down in the audience, where Alec and Akua and Pat and so many other friends and comrades sat together cheering. But pride goeth before a fall. Things were too good. Where was I doing less than I should? Had I been arrogant or proud? Surely. Was I being as kind to people as

I could be? Not always, even if it was my goal. Was I forgetting the people who helped me get where I was? I didn't think so, but maybe I'd missed something. It's true I hadn't seen my mother anywhere near as often as I could have, and that guilt was always flickering in the background, even when I felt like celebrating. As my mind raced in circles, my ear kept ringing, much to my annoyance, and everyone else's. I couldn't stop telling them when we ran into each other on the dancefloor. I fixated on the noise and it wouldn't stop.

As soon as I was able, I went to the doctor and got a diagnosis of tinnitus, for which, in my case, there was no cure. I'd have to learn to live with the constant noise, as distracting as it was. As you might imagine, spooked by health issues at the best of times, I didn't love this obvious sign of physical decline. (Nor eyesight, nor circulation, nor blood pressure, nor balance.) This wasn't existentially world-shattering on its own, but it was an hors d'oeuvre for a banquet of crises that would soon be laid out before me.

But first, back to work. I had been asked by the incandescent Michelle Obama to be part of her Reach Higher programme, so I went to the White House with a handful of other journalists to teach inner-city kids how to create a magazine. Naomi flew to DC to join Alec and me at the dinner. It felt so right, the three of us sharing that moment together. While we were there, Mrs Obama told me, 'We're all very proud of you.' I glowed. She also told me, after having watched me with the kids, that I should be a teacher. I was reminded of my juvenile beach days with my classroom full of rocks. Maybe one day, with real live humans, indeed.

A month later I had another big commemorative event to start preparing for, which would debut in June 2016. Dr Dre's category-killing headphone company Beats, along with Nick Knight, who had gone on to form the multimedia production company Show Studio, wanted to mark my twenty-fifth year in the business with a series of short films. We called them *The Seven Deadly Sins of Edward Enninful*. Nick would shoot it all, and we'd cast models who were particularly important to me to represent pride, greed, lust and all the rest. Of course, there would be Naomi and Kate, and also Jourdan Dunn, whom I have worked with nonstop since she started modelling, and Karen Elson, with whom I spent so many rewarding hours shooting with Steven. Karlie Kloss, Mariacarla Boscono, Lara Stone and Anna Ewers rounded out the cast. Its debut would be broadcast on a huge jumbotron in Times Square – a callback to my Calvin Klein days, but amplified in almost every way, as this project was all about me. Nick was as ambitious for the animation, graphics, casting and styling as I was. How had our understanding of sin evolved in the current moment? We talked about using digital collage and image distortion, with a voiceover by the rapper Travis Scott. It needed to be poetic, provocative and forward-thinking.

Fashion Month was coming to a close when we started to prep for the project. I had been particularly active as a runway stylist that season, doing at least one show per city: Diane von

Furstenberg in New York, Aquascutum in London, Giambattista Valli's second line, Giamba, and Alessandro Dell'Acqua's 21 in Milan, Sonia Rykiel and Giambattista Valli's signature line in Paris. It was Stefano Tonchi who had suggested a few weeks prior that I work with DVF, as she's known to everyone, the jet-set Belgian designer who created the wrap dress in the 1970s and has managed to remain at the head of the American fashion table ever since. Since our first one-on-one meeting that year, we became very close. We share a vision of exuberance in fashion, a joy in women, and, in moments, she's been my fairy godmother. She is so full of good advice and maternal tenderness. As always with shows, there were a lot of late nights and pressure.

I was running on vapours. I hadn't taken any time to recover from the onslaught of Fashion Month before I dipped out to Acapulco, Mexico for a commercial styling job. Aware I needed a moment of downtime, I booked a massage at the hotel just before the job wrapped. I remember lying in my room, face down on the massage table, but as the treatment ended and I raised my head to get up, when I opened my eyes, I was completely disoriented. I sat there stunned as deep black lines appeared across my field of vision. Confused, I asked them to turn the lights back up in the room, which they did, yet the lines remained. No matter where I looked, they followed my line of sight. It was as if someone had taken a thick black Sharpie pen and scrawled across everything I saw, as if my whole world was now only visible through slatted venetian blinds. I could only see in stripes.

I called Akua in a panic. 'What does this mean? Can you help me get a doctor?' Someone came to the hotel, gave me a quick exam and told me it was nothing. A champion hypochondriac such as myself was never going to accept that without seeing a specialist. That meant getting back home as soon as possible. There was a violent storm coming and some flights were already getting cancelled, but Akua managed to get me on one of the last ones. Huddled in my plane seat, slashes of black crowded my vision. I had to piece together objects in front of me, feeling my world darkening by the hour.

My optician in New York got me in for an emergency appointment and told me that I had holes in the retina of my right eye. It was due to wear and tear, he said, along with a lifelong lack of sleep and the high blood pressure that accompanied my sickle cell and thalassaemia. I was rushed to the New York Eye and Ear Infirmary in the East Village, where a lab technician prodded my eyeball with a spatula, shining a laser on it to see what was happening. It was agonising, though they told me the treatment would be less so. But the next day, I woke up unable to see anything through my right eye at all. I rushed back to the doctor, who told me the retinal tears had got worse and the eye was bleeding, which meant we couldn't operate right away. We had to wait for the bleeding to stop.

So what did I do? I put on a pair of dark glasses, got on a plane to Los Angeles and spent the best part of a week overseeing the annual Hollywood awards portfolio for *W*, one of the highest-pressure features of the year, shot by Peter

Lindbergh. I kept my mouth shut as the panic mounted, fashion directing fifty major movie stars – among them Jane Fonda, Charlize Theron, Samuel L. Jackson and Bradley Cooper – with all their attendant charisma and their publicists' demands, all the while quietly falling apart behind my sunglasses.

The day after the shoot wrapped, I went straight home to Alec in London. Getting off the plane at Heathrow, I started to see flashes of light pulsing through the darkness of my beleaguered right eye. I figured I just needed sleep, but the flashes didn't stop the next day. At the shoot for the *Seven Deadly Sins* at Show Studio's Belgravia offices, on set with Nick and the team, I asked my chief assistant Dena Giannini to look up what the flashes meant. 'Wait, what kind of flashes?' Out came the phones and the Google searches as she drafted a few other assistants into the effort. 'Flashes, but where you can't actually see through the eye?' Then everyone got very quiet. No one wanted to tell me until finally someone piped up: flashes of light through darkness meant my retina was detaching and if I didn't get surgery on that eye within forty-eight hours, I could lose my sight in it permanently.

To be honest, my vision has always been impaired, though until then it was nothing that a strong glasses prescription couldn't sort out. In fact, I had always felt that my poor eyesight had come with a side order of superpower. As the physical world could be a little fuzzy at times, it opened a gateway into my imagination, where people, places and objects would live unbridled in glorious hyper-colour focus.

When I'd sleep, elaborate visual worlds could form and tumble in my dreams. A creative person's currency is their 'vision' or their 'eye'. I was blessed with creative vision yet never had good eyesight, but the thought of losing it entirely brought with it pure existential terror. If I couldn't see, I couldn't work. Without my vision, what am I? Would I become as invisible to the world as the world would become for me?

Immediately, I called a doctor in London I had on speed dial. (Being a hypochondriac is not without its blessings.) I was willing to pay whatever it took to move as quickly as possible, and they got me into surgery that night. They stabbed a tiny gas bubble into my eye socket to hold my retina in position temporarily. Then I'd have to maintain a downward-looking posture for two weeks, my head fixed on a strange contraption, looking through a keyhole in a cushion, before a surgeon would allow any further probing.

As I was being discharged from the operating room, still in my chic hospital dressing gown, my email was blowing up with images from the *Seven Deadly Sins* shoot. They all needed my approval to keep the project on track. The producer had also emailed that I needed to return to set as soon as possible, as Nick's time was very limited and they needed to do an interview with me on camera. The nurse strapped a brace around my neck, I got into the car and went back to set. I knew I shouldn't be going to work right then, this was a crisis, but all I know – all I've ever known – is to make sure the job gets done, no matter what. I'd lived most of my adult life on a set. So back

I went. Work had always saved me from chaos, even if sometimes it brought chaos of a different kind, so even though this may seem like a very strange impulse, to me it was perfectly normal. I walked in and the team welcomed me back. We took the brace off for the filming. When I look back at that video now, all I can see is how deflated, sad and completely terrified I was.

This began a series of surgeries and recuperations – four in total – that left my head braced and downward-facing for weeks at a time. With every new foray under the knife, I prayed the doctors would do their best but still all I could do was cross my fingers. I was never given a firm prognosis for a full recovery in my right eye, but we kept at it, and then, when I wasn't in the hospital, I was strapped into one of those weird contraptions, trying to sit still, head down, waiting and brooding and worrying.

In addition to the dark fears and hopelessness, the lack of visual stimulation sent me into a deep depression. I have always had a very hungry eye and it needs to be fed with films, books, faces, nature, clothes, architecture: you name it. I'm constantly taking in references, mixing and remixing them in my mind, and then transforming them into something else. The synchronicity and randomness of people-watching in a city was part of my daily joy. Suddenly I was in isolation, proofing photos through my good eye, and then resting, unsure of how much longer the bad eye would even see at all. I was convinced it would happen to both eyes, and it very well could have. It was petrifying.

Akua cancelled freelance jobs left, right and centre, and I did what I could for *W* during my long stretches of recuperation, when I wasn't melting down emotionally. Stefano graciously offered to bring in some help on the magazine. Not just help, but the best help: the creative director Marc Ascoli and Terry Jones both took the reins to help with photoshoots and layouts while I was convalescing. Terry coming into *W* was like the return of a father. On that front, I felt very cared for.

In my unmoving terror, I listened to music nonstop. I needed some outlet for the emotional fireworks, something to cling to that would remind me of who I was in the face of so much possible erasure. I had Future's album *Beast Mode* on repeat. Trap music like his reminded me of the council estates where I grew up. In his toughness and brio, I saw my own grit and resourcefulness. And I came back again and again to Rihanna's 'Love Without Tragedy/Mother Mary'. It's a love song, but one about death and rebirth and unexpected glory and unlikely fortune, sung by a voice that had come to comfort me so many times as a friend.

> I'm from the left side of an island
> Never thought this many people
> Would even know my name

When Rihanna's voice wasn't flowing through the speakers, it was on the other end of the phone. During this period, when life slowed down to a crawl, and I worried that

I might simply disappear, she was one of the few people who checked in diligently to help keep my spirits up. 'God is good, Edward; you're going to be OK,' she'd say. 'When you're over and done with this, let's do an amazing shoot together. A kick ass cover for *W* – everyone will know you're back.' She knew I needed something to look forward to, and I knew she'd keep her promise.

When my periods of convalescence would come to an end, I'd go back to work as soon as possible, desperate to make up for lost time. *The Seven Deadly Sins* was in post-production, there were shoots coming up for *W*, and New York Fashion Week was starting again. But then I went back to the doctor in London to check in on how things were going and discovered the retina was detaching yet again. Another gas bubble. Another head brace. More worry that it would impact the other eye, which was now overstraining from having taken over the work of both of them. Would I go completely blind?

A week after my surgery it was time to go to New York for the *Seven Deadly Sins* debut. I was contractually obliged to be there, but I begged my doctor to write a note to get me out of it. He wouldn't. I was so scared to move. As much as I hated the darkness and immobility, it was better than getting on another plane. The doctor tried to reassure me, cleared me for the flight and off I went, to go and celebrate my career in Times Square, all the while fearing all of it was about to be over. At least the screening in Times Square was a roaring success. Grace Coddington and all of the models in the films joined me in a hotel suite looking out at Times Square with a direct view of the screens. I kept my sunglasses on the whole time.

And then, amid the panic and downward spiralling, an even more complete darkness descended. It was not long after this, still in New York, again face down in the dark, that my phone rang. It was Akua. I knew instantly this was the news I had most been dreading. My mother had died. The stroke that had paralysed half her body a decade before had finally taken its toll. She had been declining steadily in the past few years, and then when my parents moved out of the house where they had lived for most of our London lives, it felt as if something in her had let go – that she decided she was done with life.

I didn't know how to handle any more loss. Immediately the self-recrimination kicked in. I bitterly regretted not having been around more to have forced my mother to do her physical therapy – people were easy on her because she cried from the pain and frustration of it, but she would have listened to me if I were there to insist. I knew I didn't visit her as much as I could have. Worse, because of my ongoing eye problems, I couldn't go straight back to London to be with my family. But there would be a funeral in Ghana, and I'd find a way to be there. It was a sorrow beyond anything I'd ever felt, coupled with so much regret and guilt. I'd give anything to have her back today. I don't think a day goes by that I don't think about her and miss her still. The grieving fades to the point where you can function, but it never entirely goes away.

When I got the news of her death, it was also the kick in the ass that I needed. I knew then it was time to sort myself out profoundly, to escape this half-life I had become stuck in. As much as I would never blame my work for my own personal dysfunction, nor see work as a terrible thing I needed to escape to become whole, I knew I needed to find a healthier equilibrium, even if only so I could keep producing work that I loved at the highest level possible. I owed it to her, to honour the woman who had given me so much, planted the seeds of craft and creativity in me from the moment I was born, and nurtured me through so many years, even when family relations had felt so impossible. It was time for action.

I had heard about a specialist in New York who was the best doctor in the world for the treatment of detached retinas. The problem was, he was impossible to get an appointment with. I was obsessing over finding a way, when DVF called one day to check in on me.

'How are you doing?' she said softly.

'Not great,' I said. 'The best doctor in the world is Stanley Chang, but he's not taking any new patients.'

'But Edward, Stanley Chang is my eye doctor.'

She made the call and within a week I had an appointment. And thank God for that. Under his care, he discovered that my other eye was indeed starting to go too. Had I continued on my present course, I likely would have gone completely blind in both eyes. Dr Chang took over my treatment, and with his help, over many months, my eyes were slowly restored to functionality. In fact, I actually saw better than I ever had, albeit with a slight distortion.

I had my sight partially back – it felt like a miracle. But now I had to bury my mother. That trip to Accra was only the second time I'd been back to the country of my birth since we had all fled in the tumultuous 1980s. The moment I landed, I felt a unique comfort there. Thirty years on, the big welcoming smiles were undimmed, and so supportive, given the loss we were all there to commemorate together. The colourful fabrics, the scent of food on the warm breezes, the way the humidity made people's skin glow. All of it brought me closer to my mother, whose spirit I could sense keenly in the sea air.

I'd never seen my father so sad. 'I've lost the love of my life,' he'd say over and over to great clusters of Ghanaian friends I never even knew he had. He was so grouchy back in England, always dismissing other men for being idiots. Ghanaians aren't demonstratively affectionate with each other, so seeing him break his military bearing around these army friends told me how much he loved them, and how much pain he was in. My own sadness was inescapable and suffocating, but somehow seeing him so wrecked in his own grief made the event even more monumental.

Funerals are a big deal in Ghana. Usually there is a full week of wakes to welcome a huge number of extended family and friends. Everyone is a cousin or an uncle or an auntie, and everyone dresses their best, turning it out, because they never know if they might meet someone. (No, really – a lot of Ghanaian marriages are forged at funerals. It would make a great movie.) It was a feast for the soul, one I had been starving for, though I was too sad to take it all in. I couldn't stop thinking that if my mother had been there, everyone's dresses would have been even more beautiful. I had not been a perfect son, but she was the love of my life too.

When I wasn't with my family receiving well-wishers, I would drive around alone and revisit the scenes of my youth. There were new skyscrapers everywhere, yet it all seemed so much smaller somehow. When I saw my old primary school, I was stunned. It was tiny! The massive drainage gutters along the roadsides that I had once been too scared to jump across as a kid turned out to be less than a foot wide, easily cleared by the grown man that I had become. I made these pilgrimages unaccompanied because I wanted to be alone on my wanderings. My family and their friends seemed fine back at the hotel drinking. I assumed I also needed the space so I could indulge in my emotions by myself. But the truth was I was too devastated to cry.

Thankfully, I had an outlet for processing such a deep well of grief waiting for me back in New York. Right before Dr Chang came into my life, when life felt so fragile, I felt mentally vulnerable in a way I'd never experienced before. One moment, I'd be laughing with Dena on set, but then, invariably, the thought would creep from the back of my mind to its front that I might never see nor work again, and I'd get so quiet. Round and round this cycle went until the inevitable happened and I fell into a really profound depression. Finally Dena couldn't take it any more and told me about a therapist her mother knew. 'She looks just like Barbra Streisand – you'll love her,' she told me.

I'm English and Ghanaian, two cultures that strongly believe any hint of the blues can be easily solved with a drink and a change of subject. While I could handle the idea of dabbling in hypnotherapy on a limited basis, let's just say traditional therapy – the talky, self-interrogating kind – was not in my wheelhouse. Even with my AA experience, this was different. This wasn't a meeting where my story might be of service to someone else. Here it was just me in the hot seat, worrying that everything I was saying or describing might just be bullshit, or that I'd be judged, or that nothing would come of it, or, worse still, I'd stir up so much unhappiness that my problems would just get worse. Talking about my feelings so openly was just so American and so white. But when I walked into the doctor's office – Dena wasn't wrong, she really did look like Barbra – and sat down for our first session, I dropped my defences. Within five minutes, the doctor told me that I had post-traumatic stress disorder. 'With everything you've been through with your health, it's like you've fought the war in Vietnam.'

It took a year of twice-weekly sessions with the doctor to break down, then rebuild, how I reacted to stress and misfortune. Her approach was cognitive behavioural therapy, so our sessions were squarely focused on delineating and tracking how my mental processes worked, and how I could find my way out of them. I was happy not to talk endlessly about my childhood and instead simply concentrate on what to do with problems when they came up. When I'd go off on a worrying tangent, the doctor would point out the false assumptions and leaps in logic I was in the habit of making. She also gave me writing exercises to externalise my obsessive thinking so I could get a better grip on it. Like the twelve steps, I loved the practical application of it, and I loved that it worked. Those hours became an invaluable touchstone in the weeks and months after my mother's passing. Returning to New York, I continued my sessions and was able to throw myself back into work at *W* and for my commercial clients.

All the while I was keeping my head down, healing myself inside and out, something had been happening back in London that I had no inkling of. Early one morning in May 2016, the phone rang. It was Akua. 'You're going to get a call in the next few minutes,' she said, unusually excited. 'Whatever you do, don't pick up for anyone else. Don't miss this call.' With that, she hung up. Even early in the morning, my phone is never dormant for long, so I appreciated the warning. I put it down and watched it like a pot of water that had not yet started to boil. Five minutes later, it rang again, this time showing a mysterious London number. This must be it. I answered.

On the other end of the line was the Investiture Office of the Royal Family. I looked up at Alec with wide eyes. Huh?

'We've been trying to get hold of you,' said a well-spoken lady. Way back after I received the British Fashion Council award, apparently, my little sister had decided the time had come for a national honour. While I was getting operations and living in a world of darkness, Akua was out there gathering letters from my colleagues and putting together an application. The call I was getting now was to tell me it had been accepted. I was going to be made a member of the Most Excellent Order of the British Empire for services to diversity in fashion.

Even if, like many of my fellow Black Britons, I have complicated feelings about the British Empire's history, I have always been proud to have become an Englishman. I wasn't born one; I made myself one despite many obstacles, and perhaps that's why I felt this recognition was especially precious. This was a historically racist, colonialist institution dragging itself bit by bit into the light, and it was now choosing to reward people like me, who were working to make it a fairer and more open place. As I let the news sink in, my mind did not go to catastrophe. I did not feel like an impostor. There were no flashes of shame or worry. I was, quite simply, thrilled.

I had to keep the investiture secret for months; the Palace would make it public that June, on the Queen's birthday. That's when my father found out. My mother's death had already cracked open the door between us, just a little bit. Whenever I was in London for work, I'd started seeing him at family dinners at Akua's house in Chiswick.

Cousins and nieces and family friends would buffer us, but where there had once only been barely civil grunts, now there was a little back and forth, and the exchange of warm reminisces about my mother, shared memories of the things she used to say and do. We both missed her; we had that much in common, at least.

My father was, like many Ghanaians who come to the United Kingdom, a fierce patriot of his adopted country. So when, barely two weeks after my investiture was announced, the shocking result of the Brexit referendum came through, revealing the UK had taken the isolationist decision to leave the European Union, it hit him hard. The whole family was crestfallen. Like any nation, the United Kingdom is a country of nuance, yet for years an ever-deepening wedge had been hammered into its core by the political class and the media. It probably won't surprise you to discover that, to me and my family, one faction of the country seemed outward-looking, cosmopolitan, dynamic and modern, the country that I identified with; the other half appeared racist, small-minded, rigid and drowning in toxic nostalgia for a time before people like me – gay, immigrant, Black – had rights. My emotional reaction was that the latter side had won with Brexit, and it was heartbreaking. And it made me resolve to bring a new urgency to communicate my values in my work. I could not let the world think that the United Kingdom was as hateful and provincial and self-isolating as we appeared in this moment. My investiture became that much more important to me –

a symbol of an alternative vision of my country – and so I wanted to shout about it from the rooftops.

I was back and forth to London a fair amount in the lead-up to the ceremony that October. At least spreading my good news was one way to change the subject from the horror of Brexit. And I had outfits to get together, after all. There were multiple visits to Alexander McQueen for fittings for the suit I was having made for the ceremony. In the years since we had lost Lee, I loved seeing the company's creative director, Sarah Burton, who had worked at Lee's right hand since the beginning. She was a connection to his memory. My weight was doing its usual yo-yo, so she and I had proper work to do. I arranged for a Burberry suit for my dad, too, and hats from Philip Treacy for Alec's mum Enid and Akua.

The morning of the big day, under a classically chic grey British sky, for once I was a little less than perfectly organised. I had arrived back in London only the day before and so had to entrust assistants to make the rounds collecting everything I was to wear. In addition to the McQueen suit, there was a crisp white shirt, and a tie and braces from Anderson & Sheppard, the Savile Row house where Lee had been apprenticed as a pattern cutter back when he was practically still a kid, before he founded his own label.

It was barely controlled chaos. Charlotte Tilbury had sent some assistants to do makeup for Enid and Akua. Subrina Kidd came to do hair. Dena arrived with trays of coffee. Dryers blared and curling irons smoked. Even Ru, our beloved Boston Terrier (named after RuPaul Charles, of course), had been flown in from New York, and was curled up on the sofa as everyone got into their finery.

When you get trousers properly tailored, with buttons inside for braces, they're constructed to be significantly bigger than the actual size of your waist. But as we rummaged through all the packages, we discovered, to our collective horror, that there were no braces. Someone had either misplaced them or they never arrived, and in the madness no one had noticed. There was no way these lovingly crafted trousers would stay up on their own. Dena aimed for a solution – we're stylists; we've refitted evening gowns on rooftops and hemmed dresses in the desert, so we know how to cheat clothes to make them fit in a pinch. She suggested we take a pair of women's pantyhose and pin them to the inside of the trousers, and then have me wiggle into those, like an attached foundation garment that would hold everything up from the inside. 'How *dare* you?' I carped, and reached for a belt, which I wrapped around the outside of the trousers. They had no belt loops, but it would have to do.

I was only supposed to bring one person with me to the ceremony at Buckingham Palace, but – classic me – somehow, I managed to grow the list. In the end there were Alec and Enid, and Akua and my father, and of course, Naomi, in her own black-and-white McQueen suit, dabbing away tears with the rest of them. As I leaned forward in that grand reception hall to receive the award from Anne, the Princess Royal, she whispered to me, 'You're a brave man for bringing diversity to that industry.' I wasn't so sure about brave. It was second nature, but I thanked her and bowed, as I'd been instructed earlier by protocol officers.

Tradition dictated I was then meant to back solemnly away from the stage before turning around to retake my seat. But of course, leaning over in that awkward posture to receive my medal had caused my trousers to slip out of my belt. 'Don't let them fall. Don't let them fall,' I said to myself, silently panicking, inching backwards gingerly, staring at the plush red carpet and imagining the pastoral figures in the rich Gobelin tapestries on the walls above me rolling their eyes and sniggering. I should have listened to Dena. I said a silent prayer: Don't let me be the one getting the award for services to diversity in *fashion* with his trousers around his ankles. Don't let this proud moment turn into humiliating burlesque. Wiggle, wiggle, small step back, small step back. Somehow I made it, bottom still covered, and once out of eyeshot, I wrestled my belt back into place. Thank God I'd be changing into another McQueen suit, this one without braces, for the rest of the day.

Naomi had booked a suite at Claridge's to throw a lunch for my family. It was Sunday roast but, Naomi-style, there was also jerk chicken and rice and peas, not usually on the Claridge's menu, but of course Naomi can get anyone to do anything. I was so moved by the speeches and toasts, and then, as Naomi does, she drafted me and Alec off to her closets to help her pick her outfit for the party that night at Mark's, the private members' club in Mayfair. Eventually, she settled on a gold-sequinned column dress with a 1930s cape sleeve, once again by Sarah at McQueen.

If the investiture and the Claridge's lunch were for family, the party that night at Mark's brought the whole of London out to celebrate. We took over the entirety of the club for the occasion and filled it with bouquets of red roses. I got there early to receive people, the whole thing feeling like a terribly glamorous episode of the television show *This Is Your Life*. It was one of those rare, magical nights, and I made sure to soak up every minute. I loved my life. I built it. And the invitees who were filing through the doors not only loved me back, but had helped to make it happen. The people who came that evening made me feel ever so proud. Jonathan and Ronnie Newhouse were there first, followed by Camilla Lowther, the fashion creative agent, with her partner Charles Aboah and their daughter Adwoa, a tireless mental health activist and model whom I'd started to work with a lot. Then came the supers: Irina Shayk, Karen Elson, Kristen McMenamy, Winnie Harlow, Erin O'Connor and Lara Stone; the designers Victoria Beckham, Roland Mouret, Ozwald Boateng, Sarah Burton and Kim Jones; my beloved photographer friends Paolo Roversi, Emma Summerton and Mert and Marcus; and so many wonderful creatives from Charlotte Tilbury to Julien d'Ys and Eugene. Not everyone I wanted to be there could make it. Pat was stuck working, ditto Craig and Steven and Judy, but Madonna made it in a motorcycle jacket and leather cap trimmed with pearls. Jonathan and Ronnie hosted a table, Naomi another, Kate another, though she was characteristically late. I had my family with me at mine: Alec's parents and my father, brothers Crosby and Luther, Akua and of course Michael Boadi.

Jonathan gave a speech recalling that first Calvin job with Ronnie, and the friendship and professional rewards that grew from there. Naomi gave a speech, saying how, of all the people in the industry, I was the one person she was always willing to be there for. If that meant flying across the world for a shoot and then flying straight back again, so be it. She cried, as she usually does. And then as she took her seat, the door at the other end of the room flew open and there, finally, was Kate. Never one to let a grand entrance go to waste, with a mic in hand, she started singing 'Big Spender' in a beautifully soft and sentimental manner: 'The minute you walked in the joint,' she sang, slinking over to me, 'I could tell you were a man of distinction.' Later on that night I'd see her with her makeup bag out, giving Alec's mother a full kabuki face, complete with chopsticks pushed into her hair. The DJ Fat Tony, a fixture in our London world since the 1990s, started playing Soul II Soul's 'Back To Life'. It took me right back to the living room at Judy's, where Nellee Hooper, the impresario of the group, used to spend so many nights. Nellee was there at Mark's, too. As the first chorus of his transcendent song kicked in, someone tapped me on the shoulder and said, 'Look at your dad!'

There was Major Crosby Enninful, busting major moves. He was strutting with such military precision and focus, like he was the only one in the room. Madonna was shimmying up next to him, but he didn't even register it. I had never seen him dance like this before. After all the tension and heartache and strife we had caused each other, there we were, celebrating my accomplishments together. On this night, when we smiled and embraced each other, it was real and heartfelt. That was an achievement too.

MEGA-PHONE

London, 2017. My first Christmas party
at Vogue House for staff and contributors.

CHAPTER EIGHT

With the London celebrations complete, Alec and I returned to our flat in New York. We should have been simply full of joy, but our adopted nation suddenly felt anything but homey. The country jangled with nerves as the 2016 presidential race between Hillary Clinton and Donald Trump shuddered into its final and disturbing death throes. It was hard to escape the fear that the most influential country on Earth was about to make its own worst political mistake, just months after we had in the United Kingdom. And lo, not even two weeks after the ceremony at Buckingham Palace, when we turned the key in our front door, Donald Trump was elected president. His toxicity was all-consuming: there was his calculated race-baiting, his casual misogyny, and his chilling inclination to roll back fundamental human rights, especially for minorities. And his venal discourse about immigration was an angrier distillation of Brexit. It was like a bad dream. I was appalled watching the second of my adopted countries melt down in the most wrong-headed and reactionary way.

Experience had taught me that at moments of crisis, silence was no longer an option. I felt empowered to speak but also compelled to. Fashion is too often and too easily written off as unimportant. Yet I have always known that fashion has a unique power. When the world feels like it is shutting people down, I can touch everyday imaginations and propose an alternative way to dream. I felt a duty to offer another vision of the world, one that was less proscriptive, more thoughtful, more inclusive – an aspirational vision that anyone could see themselves in. In the political tumult of 2016, that feeling crystallised, and it is no understatement to say that this mission has become the North Star of all of my work since.

We spent most of that winter, like everyone else we knew in New York, Los Angeles and London, our mouths agape at each new indignity, working through the madness, half hoping it was just a nightmare from which we would soon awaken. Then January rolled around and Trump issued his so-called Muslim ban, barring entry to the United States for citizens of seven Muslim-majority countries. The visibly arbitrary list was enacted suddenly, and the result was mass panic – presumably exactly what its enforcers were hoping for. Lawyers rushed to airports to deliver emergency aid to travellers caught in the crossfire.

Fashion is a borderless industry that is powered by peripatetic immigrants. As I looked around New York Fashion Week in early March, I saw how 90 per cent of my colleagues living and working there were originally from other countries. We needed to make a collective statement, one Alec and I decided to work on together. We booked a studio and I called everyone I knew in the business, starting with the upper masthead at *W*, which was almost all foreign-born. We shot, for six hours, a rolling cast of designers, models, actors, editors, photographers and every other kind of creative. They filed into our studio to sit for Alec's camera and to proclaim, sometimes in English, sometimes in their native tongues: 'I am an immigrant.' There was so much anger and fear in that room, but also a profound love and respect for America, despite its current turn. We stood in solidarity. The last shot was reserved for Diane von Furstenberg, who spoke for me too when she said, a look on her face that was equal parts tenderness and sadness: 'I am an immigrant. America was very good to me.'

In the projects I took on outside of my duties at *W*, it became just as important to declare my values. Often I feel like the visual side of my work is at its most impactful when it harnesses emotions and achieves what simple words alone cannot. One of the most closely held for me, with its power to inspire and engage, is joy. We all need to express our anger, but when times are darkest, our spirits also need to be lifted. Insisting on finding joy in the middle of heartache can be a radical act of survival. (It's one that civil rights and social justice activists know only too well.) I sought out work where I could communicate joy. There was the short film I directed, cast and styled for the Gap called *Bridging the Gap*, featuring a gorgeously diverse cast of differing gender identities singing together, all wearing that great equaliser of fashion: a simple white T-shirt and jeans. And there was the 2018 Pirelli Calendar, which I had shot with the photographer Tim Walker in 2017. The iconic annual pinup book was always a feat of fashion photography. Tim, one of the great surrealists, wanted to do Alice in Wonderland with an all-Black cast. Together we went far beyond the usual Pirelli mandate (women in various states of undress) to create an alternate universe that I felt we urgently needed. Black people should see themselves in fairy tales, as they should be seen everywhere else in culture. We've been denied that for too long. (Marvel Studios had started to get it – as we were shooting Pirelli, they were shooting *Black Panther*.) The Australian model Duckie Thot, one of the faces of Rihanna's beauty line Fenty, played Alice, with a supporting cast that included Lupita Nyong'o, RuPaul, Whoopi Goldberg, Sean Combs, Adut Akech and feminist activist Jaha Dukureh.

Creative directors are understood to be primarily image people, but I was evolving into something beyond that. At this point, I'd been crafting print publications for nearly thirty years, rising from those early show reviews to helping to shape the visual language of newsstands around the world, changing the tenor of advertising, and harnessing the connectivity of video and power of digital. When all was said and done, I was happy in my work, and becoming ever more confident with using my voice to reach beyond fashion.

And yet we never know awaits us just around the corner. Unbeknownst to me, Jonathan Newhouse, back in London at the headquarters of Condé Nast International, was cooking up a plan.

It was January 2017 and I was in Paris covering the Haute Couture shows with the *W* team. Our accessories director, Karla Martínez de Salas, sat next to me in the car that was ferrying us between shows when, checking her phone, she yelped, 'Oh my God, Alex Shulman is leaving British *Vogue*!' She had been in her role as editor-in-chief for twenty-seven years when she decided the time had come to move on. It was a coveted post, though I felt the magazine had languished creatively and tonally, speaking almost exclusively to an upper-middle-to-upper-class pocket of Britishness, the denizens of a now hyper-gentrified Notting Hill and its self-reinforcing network. With every passing year the magazine felt to me like it was drifting ever further from the beating heart of the country – to say nothing of the world at large. I didn't think it reflected the Britain I knew and felt a part of. I checked my email and saw that I had missed a message from Jonathan Newhouse the previous day. It read, 'Alex Shulman is leaving *Vogue* and I'd like to talk to you.' I replied immediately that I would drop by his office in London after Couture. When I met with him a few days later, he put it plainly: 'I'm not saying you have the job, but you could have a good chance.'

This was an interesting twist. I had already been told that just before she passed from cancer at the end of 2016, Franca Sozzani had confided to Jonathan that I was the only person she thought could take over *Vogue* Italia as editor-in-chief once she was gone. Franca was such a key professional hero, and a close friend. This was deeply flattering. And I suppose, at the time, the notion of me heading *Vogue* Italia better coalesced with the general perception of me as an image person rather than a words person. (Even if that perception never took into consideration my love of literature, my devotion to narrative in all its forms, nor the fact that my first job in fashion was writing for Beth at *i-D*.)

Jonathan asked me to meet with some executives at Condé Nast and to prepare a mission statement saying, and showing, what my vision for the magazine would be. I got straight to work, pulling images from British *Vogue*'s 100-year-plus archives as well as tearsheets from my own portfolio over the years. I was inspired by the magazine's identity in the 1970s, when it celebrated a more varied array of British identities, and covered a lot more popular culture, as opposed to a fixed, insular idea of what aspiration can be.

Fashion to me is indissociable from larger cultural and political trends. But British *Vogue* was increasingly distant from the culture it claimed to represent. Sure, there was plenty of journalism in British *Vogue*, but like its imagery, the writing's worldview had honed itself to the point of being exclusionary. I wanted the magazine to redefine the notion of society, so that it was no longer a by-word for the upper crust, but simply a reference to British society at large. I wanted British *Vogue* to be a culture magazine that showed fashion alongside a much more substantial range of writing and voices. Fashion is beautiful to look at and transfixes the reader to a magazine's pages, but there's no reason why magazines should not be a must-read, page in, page out. In addition to reorganising the front of the magazine, where we'd put a new emphasis on wellness and reported stories about social issues, I proposed three main tentpoles: reflection, which meant protecting and evolving *Vogue*'s legacy of excellence; documentation, or showing the world around us in all its real diversity and dynamism; and projection, or imagining what could be possible in the future. I wanted a magazine that would speak to women like Akua – successful, discerning, opinionated, and completely missing in the pages of the magazine as it was – and embrace them like a friend. We would not be exclusive and proscriptive, but inclusive, on every page. It wasn't a popular stance in 2017, when people still freely considered women of colour – and older women, and heavier women, and non-gender-conforming women – weird and downmarket. It certainly wasn't what anyone would have expected for British *Vogue*.

As I continued to work on this mock-up manifesto, with Dena helping me to pull everything together, I started to get seriously excited. *Wait a minute,* I thought to myself as we looked over another layout, *with this job I could really shape this historic and nationally important publication and in doing so, establish a massively visible new idea for what Britishness could mean.* It would mean a big hit to my own wallet, as I'd have to give up my freelance commercial styling work to remain neutral as an editor-in-chief, but I started to yearn for the chance to make an even bigger difference in fashion and the culture at large. I knew it was time for the industry to radically re-examine itself. *Vogue* was in a unique position to help stop the issues that had plagued our industry – and society – for too long, and start dismantling them. Diversity and inclusivity were at the forefront of my mind, as well as shaking up all those outmoded notions of class that plague the UK especially. To be frank,

I was sick and tired of seeing so many people othered. And if we want to get real: I felt that *Vogue* had played some part in maintaining this state of affairs.

Meanwhile Fleet Street was going mad speculating on who would get the gig. Most of the attention was on white women already in high positions at other fashion and news publications. If I was even mentioned at all, it was at the end of a list of presumptive favourites; always the underdog. But then came the whispers. This being fashion and media, perhaps the two most gossipy industries on the planet, it took about ten seconds for someone to break my name as a front-runner, and the press went promptly nuts. Suddenly the *Daily Mail* was outside Luther's place. I was labelled 'the dark horse', and the fact that I was Black and gay was a big focus. My even being considered was presented as shocking. Hard not to see the connotations: this one doesn't belong. I was well used to it, but that doesn't mean it doesn't hurt every time.

In a boardroom in London, at Vogue House, I pitched my vision of the magazine to Nicholas Coleridge, managing director of Condé Nast Britain, alongside various suits. I was impassioned and fired up. And then, after having made my pitch, I just tried to tune out all the noise. Like when I was interviewed at American *Vogue*, my thinking was, I wouldn't get it because this is a white women's magazine. It is *Vogue* and still an honour to be considered, but c'mon, let's move on The ready-to-wear shows were in full swing, which meant I was too busy to think about much else, anyway. I was out at a party for Natalia Vodianova in Paris when my phone rang and it was DVF. 'Come over right now,' she said. 'Drop what you're doing, leave wherever you are and come to my apartment.' OK! I called my driver and asked him to take me to her place in Saint-Germain-des-Prés. She greeted me warmly and then did what we always do when DVF had advice to dispense: we sat on the foot of her bed and I took notes.

'Edward, there's a very, very good chance you're going to get this job,' she told me. As DVF is one of Jonathan's closest friends, I trusted her information. 'I want you to be very strong and make sure you're surrounded by the best people on the business side because just making a wonderful editorial product will not be enough.' It wasn't till I was back home in New York after the Paris shows that Jonathan reached out himself and asked me to come to his and Ronnie's New York apartment. Ronnie had already told me that my manifesto had blown his mind. Upon my arrival, in classic Jonathan style – meaning opaque, if charmingly so, with a wry smile – he got right down to it. 'Can you look this over and make some corrections?' he asked, pushing a document across the table to me. It was a press release announcing that I was going to become the new editor-in-chief of British *Vogue*.

It was, as they say, quite a moment. After so many months of being considered, to say nothing of a lifetime of hustling, I felt a little giddy, and was raring to go. But also, somewhere deep inside of me, there was a sense of calm. I wanted this for a reason. I had a mission.

Alex Shulman was working out a long notice period, so in the six months between the announcement of my pending arrival and my first issue, in December 2017, the reactionary British press did what it always does and had a field day. With any incoming editor-in-chief, it is standard practice to make personnel changes, and there were board-mandated reductions in head count to boot. So I came in guns blazing, or so it seemed, and the press teemed with stories, sometimes on a daily basis, about what this radical gay, Black man was getting up to. Remember this was three years before every magazine suddenly seemed to care about diversity. The global right wing had not yet adopted the word 'woke' as its insult du jour. I was truly shocked and saddened to see what I felt was the same out-of-the-box scepticism from Alex Shulman, though. After leaving British *Vogue*, she had become a monthly columnist at the influential fashion trade website *Business of Fashion* and, a month before my first issue would hit the newsstand in November, she wrote an op-ed denouncing 'the new breed of editor-in-chief'. 'The new guard of editors...' she wrote, 'will be less magazine journalists and more celebrities or fashion personalities with substantial social media followings.' Make what you will of the timing of her column. I don't recall Zadie Smith or Salman Rushdie writing for her at British *Vogue*, as they would for me, but there you go.

Then there was the story in the *Telegraph* quoting one of the editors who didn't get the post saying, 'We felt like we'd entered Crufts and the cat won'. For those of you who don't know, Crufts is a dog race. I didn't take kindly the notion that I, the lone Black person and the lone gay person, was somehow an entirely other species from the white, upper- or middle-class, heterosexual subjects who hoped to be hired – as if I had no business being in the game at all. (In general, when discussing Black people, you want to lay off the animal metaphors. We've been referred to as sub-human beasts for centuries; it's incredibly triggering.)

In the months leading up to the relaunch, I had assembled a crack editorial team, adding in some of the smartest thinkers in media brought in from the broadsheets, alongside fresh recruits from the cutting-edge style magazines. They all shared in my vision and were hungry for change. And I had a roster of new contributing editors feeding into the mission too, like Steve McQueen, whose wise counsel and cultural sensitivity always inspired me to move beyond that somewhat basic path fashion magazines can sometimes fall into. Naomi Campbell, who had booked suspiciously few British *Vogue* covers in her career, given her superstar status, was now on the masthead as a contributing editor too, bringing her wealth of cross-disciplinary contacts and fashion gravitas to our planning and brainstorming.

There was a sense of anticipation mounting. What was I going to do? How was I going to ruin this hallowed institution? Or would I give it a new shot of energy and relevance? The tongues only stopped wagging when that first issue came out, with Adwoa Aboah on the cover, shot by

Steven, of course. People finally saw the direction in which I would take the magazine: it was fresh, it was diverse, and the level of photography was higher and more ambitious than ever. It had energy and a positive, dynamic vision of British women. And it sold. As print sales have continued to shrink across the industry, British *Vogue* has continued to sell. And sell well, heading ever-upward in a fragile market. Advertising increased, too. Following DVF's briefing, I brought in Vanessa Kingori, the first Black publisher at Condé Nast, who instinctively understood the authenticity of what we were building and how exciting that vision could be to advertisers.

I've been lucky enough to have many victories since taking the job, and I can say that the sweetest ones came from sticking firmly to my convictions, despite how they went against the prevailing winds. As often as I'd heard that Black women don't sell magazines, I'd heard that Black women were not seen as capable of embodying 'luxury'. So for the August 2018 issue, I featured Oprah Winfrey dripping in diamonds, in structured couture commissions from designers like Erdem and Stella McCartney, her hair piled high like a queen. Royal style was in the air back in that May when I hired Mert and Marcus to shoot her, as Oprah was in London for the wedding of Meghan Markle to Prince Harry. For me, as well as so many other Black people, Oprah is our queen. She's more than that. As a global figure of inspiration and influence, she's more like an empress. And like an empress, she built her empire, rising from abject circumstances through the force of her talent, determination and vision. As the founder of her own magazine, a women's media juggernaut, Oprah was on her own cover, month in, month out, for twenty years, portrayed in an inviting, grounded and accessible way, like an inspiring auntie. I wanted to celebrate the pure power side of her, as one of the most formidable women in the world, and the majesty that she embodies. She loved that cover so much that she carried the magazine with her the following summer, and showed it proudly to everyone, from DVF to David Geffen. It's also prominently displayed in her office. Vanessa Kingori told me that cover was also a turning point for our ad sales, especially the jewellery companies, who thought they had died and gone to heaven.

And I could never have imagined that Meghan Markle, the Duchess of Sussex, would come to guest edit our September issue the following year. In 2019, she had become the most fascinating (and, sadly, most relentlessly chased) person in global media. We had circled each other for a while, and when we finally met, over the warmest of lunches at her then-home in Kensington Palace on the greyest of January days, a genuine connection was born as people of colour finding our way in our respective establishment bastions. Would I, she wrote to me soon after, consider allowing her to guest edit British *Vogue*?

You can imagine how quickly I said yes. The result was an edition of the magazine that would be devoted to the many facets of social justice that we called 'Forces for Change'. It was a groundbreaking statement for British *Vogue*, which had seldom given over an entire issue to celebrating activist women, as opposed to celebrities, models and tastemakers. Meghan chose fifteen activists to feature on the cover, including Greta Thunberg, Jacinda Ardern, Laverne Cox, Sinéad Burke and Jane Fonda. We put that issue together in total secrecy, with only five staffers in the loop. It meant rare, covert forays to Kensington Palace and Windsor Castle, and a ceaseless avalanche of secret comms, lest the press get wind of what we were up to and we had to junk it all. I still can't believe we pulled off. Meghan managed to have a baby between when we started that January and when the issue hit the newsstands in August. She was a phenomenal editing partner.

Our shared vision was best stated by cover star Burke, a little person and disability activist, in the lead video that accompanied the issue, directed by Alec. 'I grew up obsessed with fashion,' she said, 'because it told the world who I was in a way that I didn't have to. And yet from every touchpoint, I was excluded. British *Vogue* is challenging that.'

It felt like we had really found our groove in the public consciousness, and yet life never keeps things simple for long, does it? Just a few months after the release of the 'Forces of Change' issue, the pandemic struck. Leading a magazine under relatively calm conditions is already a herculean job, but during a time of unprecedented social, practical, even existential upheaval, it turned out to be an entirely different beast. Under lockdown, my team and I were spread out all over the city and beyond. We felt the absence of the chemistry of being together at Vogue House, functioning as one unit, but, slowly, we began getting used to the distraction of looking at our own faces during Zoom meetings, and trying to process the nonstop sensationalised headlines. We panicked for the vulnerable, for our families, our friends, our colleagues. And we wondered what our place was going to be amid the mayhem.

As the weeks of confinement turned into months, we asked ourselves constantly: what is important at this moment? Does this idea help in any way? Are we being tone deaf? During a pandemic, when everyone is indoors, when people are losing their jobs, what did it even mean to be a fashion magazine? *Vogue* readers are women (all genders, really) with families, and their lives changed profoundly. We needed to be there for them, to try to lift them up while they were panicking right alongside us.

For those fortunate enough to keep safe, lockdown slowed life down in profound ways — with nowhere to go, it meant more time to think freely, to disconnect, and to think again. Of course, even if the streets were empty, the world outside was changing furiously. Our health systems were threatened, people's livelihoods were vanishing, and our deadlines did not let up. It was a test, shepherding the magazine through this passage in history, but it would also be the ultimate proof of concept if we could pull it off: that even in an agonised world, there was always a place for beauty. Maybe more so than ever. As people saw their loved ones differently, and themselves too, there was potential for loveliness, joy and inspiration while riding that change. Nobody was going outside, although communicating with clothes started to happen in creative ways. You'd see it on the video calls that kept us all more or less connected virtually, or just at home among our own little domestic bubbles, where, as people started to lose it ever so slightly, they'd make hilarious viral videos, often in somewhat addled costume. Confinement was further proof that no matter where we are or what we endure, fashion is always there with us.

Under confinement, each issue of the magazine became a conceptual and logistical challenge, yet somewhere in the fear and madness, the run of British *Vogue* covers in that strange, scary, solitary spring and summer of 2020 felt as right as any we had ever done. For June, we shot the acting legend Dame Judi Dench for the cover, then eighty-six and the oldest cover star in the history of the magazine. With the world terrified for the fate of its elderly, the most vulnerable to Covid-19, beloved Dame Judi shone out optimistically, and the issue struck a nerve. The next month we celebrated the frontline workers whom we had come to depend on more than we could ever have imagined: the NHS staff, of course, but also delivery people, teachers, medical equipment makers, builders and food-industry workers – people who couldn't just huddle at home in safety. For that issue I commissioned Jamie Hawkesworth, a deeply sensitive photographer who started his career shooting moving portraits of real people in his home town of Ipswich. With his unique ability to penetrate into his subjects' emotions, he shifted to fashion.

He shared some of that same motivation to focus on the real world that I first developed years ago at *i-D*.

A *Vogue* shoot typically requires a dozen or more (usually far more) creatives and production staff to pull off dazzling results. Yet in March and April 2020, with lockdown restrictions at their most intense, magazine staff were legally forbidden to convene in such numbers. We secured a press pass for Jamie, and only Jamie, to travel solo, with no assistant or support team, around London on his bike, armed only with his camera. Anyone who was in London at that time will recall the extraordinary light that filled the city's streets and gardens, an almost unheard-of run of intense, blue-skied spring days that only added to the otherworldliness of what we were living through. Through Jamie's lens a history-defining portfolio of images began to take shape.

I was so moved by his pictures I decided to run three of the women, whom I considered national heroines, on a trio of covers. There was Narguis Horsford, a London Overground train driver, Rachel Millar, a community midwife at Homerton Hospital, and Anisa Omar, then a supermarket assistant at Waitrose, each shot in her work attire. It was the first time during my tenure that the magazine didn't have a model or a celebrity on the cover. The images would be a document of the times. We owed all of these people something. What could be more engaging than their heroism and service? What could be more beautiful?

For the following month, in August we didn't put people on the cover at all. Instead I commissioned landscapes from fourteen British artists, including David Hockney, Lubaina Himid, Martin Parr and Nadine Ijewere. They delivered photographs and paintings both sweeping and intimate, rural and urban, to counteract the claustrophobia of confinement. We set up a reader response called the #VogueChallenge, where hundreds of thousands readers from all over the world posted their own landscape 'covers' to social media, which I loved reposting onto my Instagram feed. We created a sense of community and escapism during this period of isolation. Readers found other readers, and through everyone's shared pictures, transported each other.

Was it a gamble not to have a cover star to sell an issue? Right after a cover featuring real women whom no one would recognise from the usual movies or catwalks? The short answer is yes. The fewer copies of an issue we sell, the less noise it makes across social media, the fewer people that it brings to our site, the more it affects our overall circulation rate, which determines everything from sales profits to advertising rates. An unpopular issue has a cascading effect that costs us money. Potentially quite a lot. But the landscape issue turned out to be a coveted item, with surprisingly strong sales. To me personally, it served a deeper purpose. Those covers in that moment provided an outlet for people to share their own environments and worldview at a time when it felt like those virtual vistas were literally all we had. It brought people together to express themselves constructively, just as we were all feeling so fragmented.

It's not that I'd been more creative during lockdown than I was before, but I certainly felt inspired to take risks in the service of that unique moment in time. The pandemic took me back to the *i-D* days, when I didn't have every resource at my fingertips, just energy and creativity and talented collaborators. It took me back even further, too, to when we made the passage from Ghana, and had to improvise on the fly, rely on our own resources and our essential trust and love in a small team.

For the September 2020 issue, with the pandemic still raging and confinement still very strict, for the first time in its history, Condé Nast coordinated a single theme across all of *Vogue*'s twenty-six international editions: hope. It was up to each editor to interpret the mandate as they saw fit. I kept considering and reconsidering cover concepts and cover stars, and dropped them just as fast. First it was a group of Gen-Z faces smiling into the future confidently; but there was too much death and tragedy every time you scrolled the headlines for grinning into the distance. Then it was a supermodel with a baby. Nice, I suppose, but no, not right now. Just a baby? Nope. Maybe it was all the other departures from the norm so far, or maybe I was having a bit of a crash, but I had never found myself feeling quite so muddled conceptually. I wasn't dreaming the cover, like I had learned to do so many years ago. I wasn't waking up and having it click.

As the days ticked down to our deadline to send the issue to the printer – a deadline that is so costly to miss, editors only do so at their peril – I kept waking up empty. The art department would mock up possibilities and I'd keep saying no. Then, on 25 May 2020, George Floyd was murdered by a Minneapolis police officer, and the world emptied out into the streets in protest.

For me, like for many other Black people, Floyd's murder was a moment of gut-wrenching catharsis. On the one hand, there was the pain in acknowledging that it took watching a video of a helpless man die with a police officer's knee on his neck for the world to act. On the other hand, the response was bigger and broader and more international and fundamental in depth and scale than at any other moment in history. If you were Black and had a platform, it was not the time to stay quiet. To be honest, if you were not Black and didn't have a platform, it was not the time for silence. No matter your race, it was time to speak up. And keep speaking up. It still is.

As I was planning the September issue, I was also organising virtual round tables, and having crisis discussions with Black leaders in other industries like Trevor Noah, Kendrick Sampson, Virgil Abloh, Oprah Winfrey and the Duchess of Sussex. And I set a precedent of urgency for the content of the website. I have never been into lip service. I wanted to be clear with the tone that British *Vogue* would take from the first moment. It was important that my voice, and the voice of the magazine, be heard loudly, and globally.

The protests went on all summer, many of them outside Alec's and my flat, and we were out marching like everybody else. But back in May, even before their persistence and efficacy at prompting real change would be fully understood, I was struck by how the entire world came to support my race. (This extends to Condé Nast, which responded to the increased awareness by creating a diversity and inclusion programme that included pay and hiring transparency.) There were bigots refusing to be silent whilst we grieved, but for the most part I felt unity. The young generation showed up unreservedly, with passion and fury, among my team at *Vogue*, on social media, in every conversation I was having. Seeing those young people fuelled by rage and purpose gave me goosebumps. And hope.

So there it was. Hope. Finally, it clicked. For September, I'd do a black-and-white gatefold of portraits of social-justice activists from the United States, Africa, Asia and, of course, the UK, representing the hope of the moment. It borrowed conceptually from 'Forces for Change' and our frontline workers issues in its insistence that everyday people were as beautiful and inspiring as any celebrity. And what could be more optimistic than activism, people putting their lives on the line to make the world a better place? Besides, the biggest, most connected civil-rights movement the world has ever seen had to be documented. Like Nina Simone said, 'An artist's duty ... is to reflect the times.' I wanted to put one theme front and centre: the collective will to make things better.

Now all we had to do was pull off thirty-eight socially distanced photoshoots across five cities: London, Atlanta,

New York, Chicago and Los Angeles, while arranging remote imagery of other advocates around the world. In a week. With ever-evolving travel restrictions.

The casting came together almost instantly. I am lucky to have a diverse team that includes minorities and allies working for me at British *Vogue*, and everyone threw themselves passionately into the project, at extremely short notice.

For the main cover we booked Adwoa, whose mental health and feminist activism credentials couldn't have been more relevant to a pandemic that placed women, in particular, in danger at home. She posed with Marcus Rashford, the Manchester United star who successfully lobbied the UK's Conservative government to cover free meals for low-income, locked-down kids, who depended on their daily school lunches. Inside the gatefold there was Janet Mock, the television writer, director and trans activist, as well as Joan Smalls, the Puerto Rican model who had just pledged half of her considerable salary for the rest of 2020 to organisations affiliated with Black Lives Matter. (Joan is one of the highest-paid models in the world; that was not a small gesture.) There was Patrick Hutchinson, a demonstrator at a Black Lives Matter rally in London who carried a white-supremacist provocateur to safety, Jane Elliot, the veteran anti-racism educator behind the 'brown eyes/blue eyes exercise', and Bernice King, a minister and one of the daughters of Martin Luther King, Jr., who heads his foundation, the King Center. I assembled five up-and-coming Black photographers on two continents and we got to work. The majority of the subjects dressed themselves, which is a statement in itself.

Magazine covers are the most coveted real estate you can imagine for fashion houses, and designers who pay to advertise expect to see their key pieces worn by cover stars. In magazine terms, for September issues, the importance of what clothing appears on the cover is about as crucial as it gets. We did style Adwoa and Marcus, but we seized the opportunity to deepen the message, and have them wear minority designers who weren't all advertising with us. But with the gatefold and inside portfolio, we let thirty-seven golden opportunities for advertising credits go up in smoke. This is a nightmare for a publisher or market editor to deal with; however, to me it was a moment that had to be authentic right down to the seams of the clothing. It wasn't about clothes as objects of desire, it was about what fashion can communicate in this moment, as an extension of a wider purpose. To me, it was more important that each of these activists could shine as their true self. To dress them up would be to put them in costumes. Sometimes you have to know when to leave things alone. I simply asked each of them to wear something that made them feel themselves. For Jesse Williams, the American actor and activist, it was a tracksuit. For Janet it was a white blazer and T-shirt. Everyone approached it differently.

The opportunities to turn up the volume of our megaphone at *Vogue* continue to grow, some of them to an almost surreal level. I've interviewed Prince Charles about his sustainability efforts in fashion, and signed on as global ambassador of the Prince's Trust, the organisation that helped so many members of my working-class family get professional training. On 11 September 2020, I was on the cover of *Time* magazine. 'Fashioning Change', read the headline of that venerable institution of American journalism. 'Edward Enninful shows the power of inclusion'. That I'm considered a standard-bearer only fills me with a greater sense of urgency. OK, everyone, I've got your attention. I promise you I'm not going to waste your time.

The day that *Time* dropped, still under conditions of confinement, I was doing a virtual cover shoot with Beyoncé that we had to figure out on Skype. She made a point to thank me, 'for all you stand for. It feels so good to be doing this cover with you, for you, for a Black editor.' We talked about how we shared a similar work ethic and a similar motivation to challenge the status quo, but always uplift at the same time. Nothing fights the power like pure excellence. 'You're a good person,' she told me, for staying up till four in the morning so I could direct the shoot. Good, sure, why not. Really I just didn't want to miss the chance to work with another queen, one of the most rewarding perks of my job.

And yet, for every up there is a down, a lesson I experienced for the millionth time on my first day back at the office. Lockdown restrictions having eased a little, I was on site to close the issue, British *Vogue*'s big political statement on hope that I had spent every hour of my days, and many of the nights, toiling over. Arriving at the offices in Mayfair, I was on my way into the building with my little *Vogue* tote bag holding my laptop, running through my mental checklist of which layouts I wanted to see first, which calls I needed to prioritise, when all of a sudden I was stopped in my tracks. Literally. Arriving at the door of Vogue House I was confronted by a security guard, a white woman, who looked me up and down and refused to let me in the building. I thought that was strange, so I opened the door myself and carried on past. As I did, she walked towards me. I thought she would ask, 'How can I help you?' But no, she looked right through me and bellowed, sternly: 'LOADING BAY.'

'Excuse me, what did you just say?' I asked her.

'DELIVERIES GO THROUGH THE LOADING BAY.'

Not today, Satan.

'I'm the fucking editor of this magazine,' I told the guard, incredulously. She looked like she was going to die on the spot. She apologised profusely, but that just made it even worse, as if she could have profiled any other Black person, and she was only apologising to me because I was in a position to get her into trouble. I went upstairs, sat down at my desk and called human resources. I told them what happened. Then I told my team. The Black and Brown *Vogue* staffers told me it didn't surprise them. Did it surprise me? I guess not. It certainly infuriated me.

Later, I posted about the experience on social media. The majority of the comments were supportive. But there were also plenty of takes like, *Maybe you should have been wearing a suit?*

Or: *Maybe your ego's just too big because you weren't recognised?* In short, the definition of gaslighting. Did people honestly think that day was the first time I had been profiled in my life? It was maddening, coupled as it was with the toxic irony of it happening on the very day we were putting to bed our most important and optimistic issue yet, lifting up some of the brightest lights in the search for justice for Black people.

As a Black person in the fashion industry – as a Black person on planet Earth – I have been profiled more times than I can count. I have thick skin at this point; I can handle it. But I won't stand by and allow the next generation to go through the same kind of treatment if I can help it. And unlike the younger kids who work in my building, and most younger kids in their places of work, I have the power to do something about it. So I went public. It would be unthinkable to me to just say, 'Well, I've arrived', and to leave them to fend for themselves. If I'm not here to lift up the younger generation, then what the hell am I doing?

And it's not just the young I feel compelled to look out for. My mind is always on the job ahead. These past few years have been an extraordinary and fast-paced time of change, and I am grateful for the inroads that have been made. When I look at the catwalks now, at advertising, at the covers of other magazines, and see a beautiful array of faces and bodies and identities, it's not that I feel it's all due to me, but I do clock my part in that process. In the space of my career so far, I have gone from singing in the wilderness to helping achieve a reset in the fashion industry's entire tone. I'm incredibly proud of that.

But I will never stop asking, 'What's next?' These days, when I look at other media platforms and teams and certain fashion houses, I see the surface effort, and appreciate parts of it, but now it's time for more. My first language is still fashion. I know it can seem like a mysterious, hoity-toity world to many, but it touches so many lives. Fashion wields traditional power in terms of economics and jobs, but its soft power also has tremendous influence. And I'm not sure soft power has ever been more crucial. Fashion's ability to shape conversations and empower individuals and communities will only become more potent in the years to come. Fashion is a language in and of itself and it deserves its own, much deeper reckoning. One that is global, that has the emotional empathy and authenticity to truly connect with people, as well as the digital smarts to see that evolution through and give it its widest possible reach. And it must become sustainable if it's going to be a part of our solutions going forward. We've done some good work. But it is time for fashion to embrace its future.

On a shoot day recently, these thoughts were much on my mind. I was overseeing the cover of British *Vogue*'s February 2022 issue: a group portrait of a superstar set of African models shot by the Black Brazilian photographer Rafael Pavarotti. African models are having a legitimate moment in fashion. Dark-skinned girls like Adut Akech and Anok Yai have been shining in prime spots, opening Prada shows, getting

Estée Lauder contracts, and not just as the only Black girl in a rainbow shoot, thrown in for extra credit. These women are stars in their own right. The fate that befell Naomi or Alek Wek of being the one Black girl in a fashion show is in the past where it belongs. Could it be that casting directors are slowly learning to see differently? That model scouts are finally realising it is worth their time to go to Lagos as well as Tallinn? Well, I wasn't going to miss the chance to celebrate this moment.

No one working today better plunges into the mystery and transcendent beauty of dark skin as deeply as Rafael, who was born in a Brazilian rainforest and grew up in a remote corner of the country. When he was a kid, he'd trek for miles to the nearest internet café to look at pictures of John Galliano's shows for Christian Dior. (There's something to be said about the singularity of purpose that it takes to work in fashion when you never had access to it growing up.) As a photographer, Rafael has a sharp graphic sense and love of Black skin, but he foregoes the Banania ironies and exoticising tendencies of his predecessors and inspires layers of emotions out of his models. Yes, the February cover stars were almost all very dark-skinned, though that was where their similarity ended. Rafael and I wanted to look deeply where other people might have just ticked a box. In these pictures, we see the fierceness of Adut, the wide-eyed wonder of Anok, the quiet joy in Amar Akway, the androgyny of Majesty Amare.

February is an issue when fall and winter clothes, historically considered the chicest and most fashion-forward, make their last big statement before spring kicks off in earnest. Too often Black models are consigned the happy, skimpy, colourful summer collections, not the directional avant-garde of the cold-weather months. We would fix that. We had noticed a lot of black, and the return of the big, broad shoulder, and we wanted to see these proud, edgy clothes on proud, strong African women, each with their own interior world to express.

Together, Rafael and I spent days and nights talking about inspiration. We weren't going for naturalism, no short Afros. We wanted stylised, and we wanted images worthy of my mother, who came into her own in the 1960s and 70s, when African countries were flourishing in independence and the women were fierce. We didn't want smiles. We weren't trying to coax anyone into comfort. We wanted the proud, regal beauty I dreamed about as a little boy looking up at the walls of Dolly Dots. We looked at the portraits of Malick Sidibé and went deep on the Supremes and Eartha Kitt. We wanted retro-pressed hair and stiff spines, structured and serious.

On the day of the shoot, Rafael – who is still in his twenties, but a very old soul – called the cast and crew together into a circle and asked for a moment of silence. He wanted to ground us all together, so we could focus on our shared purpose before flipping the switch and going into set mode. It was profound to be there, the excitement radiating off us, pounding through our hands. When I opened my eyes, I looked around and saw all those women together, many of them raised in refugee camps, none of them having imagined as little girls where they would be on that day, exemplars of the beauty of the moment, the apex of a new fashion elite.

This was fashion. It wasn't Black fashion or African fashion: it was high fashion, major designers, the crest of the innovation, embodied and interpreted by African women. And it was brought to you by *Vogue*, the arbiter of and authority on what fashion means to the world at large. So I kept the words on the cover of this issue simple and authoritative: 'Fashion Now: First Look at the New Season and the Faces Shaping 2022'. When I debuted the cover photo and a few images on Instagram, I wrote a note calling an end to the idea of tokenism for ever. To me it felt as if I was completing the circle that started with the Black Issue of *Vogue* Italia back in 2008. This was not a special issue. It was fashion in its own right, leading the season, for everyone's pleasure.

I wasn't prepared for the reaction. After all the groundbreaking covers, the celebrities – Madonna, Kate, Naomi, Lady Gaga, Adele, you name it – this cover got the biggest response of them all, apart from just one other: our radical makeover of Billie Eilish. As the women were all so dark, with Rafael's blue-toned lighting showing them even darker than they might have appeared in standard daylight, it tipped off a fierce debate on colourism that I was happy to see. (Light-skinned beauty is not the only Black beauty.) But mostly, the feedback was heartfelt and celebratory. Scrolling down the responses were a sea of emojis; flames, heart eyes, hearts, hearts, hearts, so many of them black. And then there were the written comments that told me how much these pictures meant.

'I've never seen anything more beautiful, I want to cry.'

'This is the cover we were waiting for.'

'This gonna set so many people free.'

And that's the whole idea. That's it right there. Because beauty can set us all free if we let it. If you need any more proof of that, here I am.

THANK

Alec Maxwell
Darnell Strom
Albert Lee
Meredith Miller
Alexis Kirschbaum
Alexandra Marshall
Christopher Richards
Lauren Whybrow
Stephanie Rathbone
David Mann
Genista Tate-Alexander
Fran Owen
Mari Yamazaki
Anna Massardi
Office Of Craig
Vimbai Shire
Alyson D'Amato
Casey Denis
Dena Giannini
Terry and Tricia Jones
Judy Blame
Emily Hallie
Sam Mitchell
Giles Hattersley
Afua Hirsch
Grace Coddington
Salman Rushdie
Naomi Campbell
Kate Moss
Steven Meisel
Luther Enninful
Kenneth Enninful
Wilhelmina Enninful
Akua Enninful

Crosby Enninful (junior)
Crosby Enninful (senior)
Zoe Edmund-Jones
Yasmine Hanni
Deborah Ababio
Idris Elba
Ronnie Newhouse
Jonathan Newhouse
Craig McDean
Pat McGrath
Michael Boadi
Jimmy Moffat
Steve McQueen
Paul Hunwick
Simon Foxton
Nick Knight
Steven Klein
Rafael Pavarotti
Misan Harriman
Jamie Hawkesworth
François Goizé
Stas May
Anita Bitton
Oprah Winfrey
Dean Baquet
Joseph Kahn
Eugene Souleiman
Mert Alas and Marcus
Piggot
Domenico Dolce
Stefano Gabbana
Simona Baroni
Rihanna Fenty
Beyoncé Knowles

Vanessa Kingori
Trevor Noah
Emma Summerton
German Larkin
Matt Brooke
Wolfgang Tillmans
Jason Evans
Franca Sozzani
Anders Madsen
Campbell Addy
Nicole LePage
Ariela Goggi
Virginia Smith
Felicia Garcia-Rivera
Jack Borkett
Beth Summers
Eniola Dare
Uwe Doll
Natasha Poonawalla
Guido Palau
Rana Reeves
Iman Abdulmajid
Diane Von Furstenberg
Jannico Meyer
Charlotte Tilbury
Philippe Brutus
Riccardo Tisci
Virgil Abloh
André Leon Talley
Bethann Hardison
Michael Pestana
Juergen Teller
Dovile Teller

YOU TO

IMAGE

CREDITS